Table of contents

Prologue

What does the word 'trans' mean to you? A term picked up from magazines, newspapers, the internet? A way of describing a colleague – maybe even a friend, or family member? A phenomenon affecting other people? Or, perhaps, a facet of who you think you might be?

When I work with organisations to provide trans diversity training, I always begin by asking for other people's definitions. Inevitably, writing them up, I run out of space on the whiteboard. Suggestions for what 'trans' means includes: people who were assigned one sex at birth (male or female) who medically transition to the other, people who live as the opposite sex without surgery or hormones, people who combine or blur sex and gender categories, and people who cross-dress. Participants suggest words and meanings: trans-sexual to mean someone who has or wants to transition, transgender to indicate a wide variety of unusual gendered experiences, and genderqueer, gender-neutral and non-binary to mean someone who complicates the simple division of female and male, combining or denying these categories.

All of these ways of being can be included in the word 'trans'. Any person who has had to challenge or change the sexed and gendered labels placed upon them at birth to honour their true selves can, by their own or others' volition, find themselves under this trans umbrella. The category of trans can be an uncomfortable place to be, filled with the fears society has about disruption, fitting in, danger and change.

It is also a place filled with unlooked for knowledge, new experiences, new perspectives, and unanticipated joy.

This is a book about gender – how we all live it, how we think about it, why we do and think what we do. It is also about how some of those things have changed and will change. It is a book about what it is to be trans, to be a woman or a man or a person who is neither, in different times and in different places. It is about our gendered words, and how those words lead to the concepts, laws and categories that shape our frequently conflicting realities: our families, our love lives, our place in the world. It is a book about my journey through gender, sex, selfhood – and, if you want it to be, about yours.

Throughout this book, I'm going to break down the most common myths about trans lives: panic about 'sex changes' for young children, the fear of trans people in bathrooms and changing rooms, and the assumption that being trans is a faddish new trend. A little knowledge is a dangerous thing; luckily, we have a wealth of information about what it is to be trans, and how the world is changing and growing in response to the challenge of trans lives.

Inevitably, when we talk about being trans we have to talk about transphobia. It is hard to live it: it can be hard to read it. It is so tempting to become defensive, to shut down and try to shut it out, to ignore it until it goes away.

But we – all of us – cannot fix this problem until we look it square in the face. And what it is that we gain from embracing the truth of trans existence is so great, so important, that this is a challenge we must take on. We cannot have the good without tackling the bad – and the good is better than we have ever been taught to expect.

I came out as trans half a lifetime ago. In all these intervening years, I have had my share of hardships, but I have never regretted the decision to tell the truth about my gender. I cannot put a price on the wonder of being at peace with who I am, and of living my life as my whole, authentic self. I believe we all deserve a chance at that happiness.

Opening ourselves up to the trans experience – whether or not we ourselves are trans – means embracing a new way of seeing the world. It requires trust, empathy and imagination. It is not a one-way process, but a journey we are all on together.

This is one book, and one story, out of millions. This is a work in progress.

1

The Production of Ignorance

Daily Express, January 2011: '"Half Man" gets new breasts (and guess who's paying £78k).'

Courier Mail, October 2014: 'Monster Chef and the She Male.'

The Times, February 2016: 'I'm just a bloke, says sex-change soldier.'

Daily Mail, October 2015: 'Children as young as FOUR being given transgender lessons.'

We're often the butt of the joke: The *Sun*'s 2011 game 'Tran or woman?'. There's an air of the freak show about us, an invitation to peer into the bizarre realities of our lives: 'Transsexual, 44, elects to die by euthanasia after botched sex-change operation turned him into a "monster".' Even when the intent is celebratory, we are marked out as different and strange: CNN's list of the most influential people of 2014 described actress and advocate Laverne Cox as 'The Gender Bender'.

Here are a few of the things the media shows, and has shown, trans people to be: confused, deceitful, delusional, damaged, predatory, brave (sometimes), pitiable, pathetic. A punchline, a warning, a mistake.

Here are a few of the things I am: a singer, a teacher of music, a good (if forgetful) friend, a loving child and grand-child, a loved and loving partner. I am a doctoral student, a decent cook, too ambitious, too anxious, a composer of all kinds, and someone who tries, at least, to be better than my worries would have me be. And I'm also transgender.

Rarely has that disconnect between trans reality and its interpretation been so clearly shown as with the publication of British journalist Richard Littlejohn's 2012 'character assas-sination' of primary school teacher Lucy Meadows. Meadows was not a public figure. She hadn't contacted the press to sell her story, hadn't issued a release, hadn't promoted herself via social media. It didn't matter. 'He's not only in the wrong body ... he's in the wrong job' the headline announced, accompanied by a photo of Meadows on her wedding day, back before she had transitioned. Referring to her as 'he', Littlejohn warned that Meadows' mere presence would have a 'devastating effect' on her young pupils. '[Meadow's previ-ous name] is entitled to his gender reassignment surgery, but he isn't entitled to project his personal problems on to impressionable young children.'

As a teacher of students ranging in age from five years old to fifty, this was the first I had heard about projecting my personal issues onto my pupils. My lesson plans focus mostly on technique, creativity and personal growth, with a side order of self-confidence boosting and chatting about musical history. My private life doesn't come into it. I don't hide who I am with my students and their families, and neither do I dwell on it; the fact that I am trans is as fundamental as any other part of me, but far less important in this context than my knowledge of vocal production and how best to play staccato. I teach for many reasons, but most of all because my own music teachers gave me so much, and I have a debt to repay through sharing the joy of making music. It makes no sense to me that my support of my young students would somehow rob them of their innocence, nor can I interpret the work I put into others' learning as 'selfish'.

In the end, Littlejohn need not have worried. Lucy Meadows did not remain in her job for long. Three months after transitioning, in March 2013, she killed herself.

Ascribing a single cause to any suicide is both dangerous and disingenuous. Lucy Meadows, like many of us, struggled under multiple burdens. But it is also true that the coroner who investigated her death, Michael Singleton, believed that the press had played a role. Speaking at the inquest, he said: 'Lucy Meadows was not somebody who had thrust herself into the public limelight. She was not a celebrity. She had done nothing wrong. Her only crime was to be different. Not by choice but by some trick of nature. And yet the press saw fit to treat her in the way that they did.' Finishing his statement, he turned to the gathered reporters and said: 'And to you the press, I say shame, shame on all of you.'

How can it be that both trans people and the journalists who write about us believe ourselves to be talking about the same subject, and yet have such wildly different beliefs, words and ways of speaking? Differences so vast that the same life can be deemed both worthy of respect and worthy of public ridicule, an inspiration and also a disgusting threat? Differences that play out not just in the media, but in how wider society treats trans people?

These writers are recording the trans 'debate' in one language, and trans people like me are speaking the realities of our lives in a totally different tongue.

How are we meant to reach the people who are not trans, when they are primed to believe the opposite of how trans people live our actual lives? How much longer must we misunderstand each other, trapped in the falsehoods created by the production of ignorance?

I was first introduced to the concept of 'the production of ignorance' at an early music conference in 2015. The focus of the day was on women composers and music-makers in Western history, and of particular interest to me was the question why, after celebration and acceptance in their own eras, after decades of careful research, re-evaluation and performance, so many people, even musicians, believe that there were no women composers before the twentieth century. In one of the question and answer sessions musicologist Melanie Marshall put forward an answer that clarified not only this problem, but which also explained to me so much about popular knowledge and general confusion over gender issues. Referencing the work of Nancy Tuana, Marshall described the concept and process of the production of ignorance: it is not just the absence of knowledge that keeps a truth from being widely known and accepted, it is also the active production of ignorance that suppresses that truth. It is not only that we are unaware of the many women composers throughout history: we are actively taught that there were none, or certainly none worth bothering about.

Similarly, it is not that trans people are ignored entirely, but that what we are taught as fact can often obscure and distort the truth in a way that even silence could not.

Not that silence is the solution, even if it were still possible. Much has been made of the 'trans tipping point', from the front cover of *Time* magazine to the daily, twice daily, articles in English-language media throughout the world. It is undeniable that the media is having a trans moment. Interviews with trans adults, features on trans children, possible changes in legislation that would help trans people, definite changes in legislation that will hurt us, another trans death in prison, another trans person in custody, a gender fluid celebrity, a charity campaign. Some of this content is incredibly good, and some is just incredible. In an age of declining sales of offline media, the end of physical newsprint and the importance of clickbait ad revenue, there's a particular winning formula when it comes to trans issues: anti-trans opinion piece (as shocking as possible), report on the hurt caused by said piece (search Twitter), pro-trans rebuttal (in the same paper). Rinse and repeat on a regular basis. It doesn't matter why people are reading – agreement, rage or the hope of titillation – so long as it sells. And, right now, trans sells.

When we apply the concept of the production of ignorance to this cycle we can see why and how it plays out.

To learn how to learn about trans people, about the ways in which what we know about gender is shifting and growing, we first must unlearn.

*

The question I am most often asked about being trans – on the internet, in the pub, on the bus, at work – is the one I most dread answering. Sometimes it's delivered through euphemism, sometimes crudely, and worst of all by a groping, uninvited hand. 'Have you ... you know?' or 'so you're ... post- or pre-op?'. It's colleagues I barely know asking me what kind of genitals I have and whether I'm going to change them – and, if so, how – and strangers recoiling in horror, because 'I don't know what you have down there'. This, for them, is *the* defining point of being trans: the 'sex change', the 'op'. Never mind that there are many different kinds of medical treatments that trans people may undergo, if it's right for us, if we have the money, if our medical systems allow it. In the popular imagination there's a singular operation, and a violent, last-option one at that. Various forms of detailed, sensitive reconstruction work become 'lop your tits off' and 'cut your cock off'. It's the supposed proof of being trans and, more than that, it's everybody else's business.

What we experience on a day-to-day basis we see modelled by the media: documentaries, interviews, movies, TV shows. It's the triumphant finale of 2005 film *TransAmerica*: Felicity Huffman sliding her hands between her legs in relief at the absence of her (much publicised prosthetic) penis. In 2015 documentary *Girls to Men*, the film-makers framed the stories of their young trans masculine protagonists in terms of their journey towards genital surgery. Gory surgical footage and close-up cock shots; that the audience should become a voyeur is a given, because they, somehow, have not only the right to know but the right to gawp. Even when a trans person has not volunteered the information, the topic is considered fair game – more than that, essential. Watch the

2014 interview of Carmen Carerra and Laverne Cox by Katie Couric: the ease with which Couric asks about her interviewees' genitals, and her confusion at being denied an answer.

For many of the people who ask, the fact that a ready answer might not be forthcoming is baffling. After all, isn't that how being trans is meant to work? Someone realises that they're 'trapped in the wrong body', then gets that body overhauled and emerges a new person. It's everything we've been taught from the earliest ages: women have vaginas and men have penises. If we, trans people, want public acknowledgement of who we are then, the argument goes, we should accept the public judgement of our genitals.

If we were to take another example, and apply the same rules, it becomes obvious just how inappropriate and harmful this trope is. For some (not all) trans people, one element of being trans is the physical process of transition. It can be joyful, it can be painful, it can be messy and it can involve surgery. The same could be said of parenthood. Conception, pregnancy and childbirth are necessary parts of making a family for the majority of people. Like medical transition, it is vital that we're educated about these processes if there's a chance we'll find ourselves personally affected. And luckily, in both of these cases, the medical information is freely and easily available online, through public health initiatives, in libraries, and from the relevant medical authorities.

But it would *never* be appropriate to approach a new mother in a café and say: 'so did you rip your vagina giving birth to that one?' When greeting a colleague returning to the office after maternity leave we don't ask if we can examine the stretch marks and possible scars, or ask about haemorrhaging and post-natal incontinence. If we're close friends or family, we might well talk about the most personal physical aspects of creating and delivering a baby – the same is true of transition. But the need to be honest and close with our loved ones doesn't make the intrusion of strangers okay.

The second problem is that of language. Obvious transphobic language in the media – and in the wider world – is hard to ignore. Even those people who are themselves transphobic could hardly pretend that Julie Burchill's infamous 2013 column was inoffensive, with her descriptions of trans women as 'bedwetters in bad wigs' and 'dicks in chicks clothing'. You don't need to know anything about trans people to know that referring to us with insults is cruel.

What worries me more is the trend to describe all transrelated language as somehow 'made up', 'difficult' and too 'PC' to be allowed.

When I'm asked to give a talk, write an article or deliver training on trans issues, I'm well aware of the fact that the words I use won't be familiar to everyone, and am happy to explain. 'Trans' is the word I favour, as it has the broadest and most flexible definition: any person who, in some way or combinations of ways, has found that how they experience their gendered self does not fit with the gender and sex they were assigned at birth. 'Cis' is the antonym of trans; just as we cannot describe being gay without having a word for straight, we need a word to describe experiences which are *not* trans, as well as experiences which are. These words are blunt instruments, designed to give a rough understanding of the ever-changing world we find ourselves in; tools to help us to understand and challenge the ignorance and prejudice between us. They will change with time, and new words will take their place: humans are quite remarkable in their capacity to learn new words. For example, we now use the word 'you' in both the singular and the plural: not so in Early Modern English. In the past twenty years the word 'internet' and all its related terms and add-ons (including the term 'add-on') have entered into daily, unremarked usage. As a teacher, I'm constantly introducing words that are new to my students: rubato, cantabile, légèrement. When new words can bring us closer to something we want to say then we are all too happy to learn them. And this is why I'm suspicious of the claim that trans-related words are too much, too hard and of no use.

Even when a word has been in usage for a long time, those who are suspicious of what that means in terms of gender are quick to claim that the change is too fast. 'They' has been used as a singular pronoun in English for hundreds of years; we find examples of the singular they in the works of Shakespeare, Austen and Swift. But trans people like me, who use the pronoun 'they' as a gender-neutral alternative to 'he' or 'she', are often mislabelled in the media by editors who struggle with its usage. By implying that trans people are faddish and difficult about words, writers can cast aspersions on the validity of our language – and of our selves. By claiming that our words are too hard to understand, the media perpetuates the idea that *we* are too hard to understand, and suggests that there's no point in trying.

Learning how to talk about trans people is not difficult, and doesn't require any specialist knowledge. Just as you would in any other situation, you just have to reflect back the words a person uses about themselves. Wanting to be referred to in an accurate and respectful way isn't a trans-specific thing, but a cornerstone of polite society. I don't call my Jewish friends Buddhist. It's the same with trans people. Use the right names, use the right pronouns, and don't fall for the line that we're too difficult for our own good. I know many cis people who are so nervous about getting it wrong that they're scared to try to get it right, but it's okay to ask. I would far rather someone asked me what pronoun I use than tried, out of embarrassment, to guess, and got it wrong.

The final problem of the framing of trans lives so often recycled by the media is perhaps the hardest one to see. So often it is the only way in which trans people are included in the media at all. Less obviously pernicious, but still dangerous, is the way in which trans people are only featured when *being trans* is the story.

The most obvious, and most egregious, example in recent years must surely be in the press treatment of scientist Kate Stone. Dr Stone was gored by a stag in a freak accident in late 2013; as someone who had not sold her story, who was not in the public eye, she had no reason to suspect that her accident would hit the news. And yet she, and her family and friends, were confronted with headlines such as 'Sex swap scientist in fight for life' and 'Deer spears sex-swap Kate'. Speaking to the *Guardian*, Stone explained: 'I have no regrets about the accident. I have never for one moment thought, "Why me?" But some of the reporting was horrendous. The media doorstepped my family, my friends and colleagues. On radio, one 'expert' was asked, 'Was Kate gored by a stag because she was transgender?''

This is an extreme example, for sure. Most of us will never experience this kind of treatment, although more trans people have experienced door-stepping than you might expect. Stone sought help from the Press Complaints

Commission and, eventually, the intrusive stories were withdrawn. But the broader point – that being trans is, in its own right newsworthy – impacts on the way all trans rights are framed.

When I was first starting out as a performer, I was shocked by the number of people in the media who were more than happy to write about me, but not as a musician: only as a trans sob story. I refused to provide 'before' and 'after' pictures, to give away the personal details of my life: most of the press interest disappeared. We're forced into a double bind; if we're to speak honestly about who we are then we must have the freedom to talk about being trans, but we cannot be reported honestly if being trans is the *only* aspect of our lives discussed.

I know many trans people who have spoken to the media about what it is that they *do* – their professional expertise, their artistic ventures, their latest projects – and are later confronted with a final copy that cuts out all of that detail for a clichéd trans narrative that has nothing to do with the actual life of person featured. Through this framing we are made to look like attention seekers and oddities. If we don't mention being trans, we risk one of two options. If, like me, we are visibly different, then we are usually pressed to talk about it. If we are not seen as trans, we run the risk of accusations of deception, of a scandalous 'reveal', if we don't announce that we are trans from the get-go.

As in the media, as in everyday life. Without being able to talk about being trans, I can't speak about how I have been made to suffer for it, and also what I have learnt through those experiences. I can't make things better by being silent. But neither can I speak about every other part of my life – live every other part of my life – if other people focus only on my transness as something shocking and different.

It has to be our choice to talk or not talk about being trans, and – whether we talk about it or not – we still need to be recognised as whole, complex people. Our lives are truncated when we are seen only through the stereotypes of others, and we waste so much time struggling against those constraints. Whether it's on the front pages or in the workplace, 'being trans' is never the most interesting thing about us. Accept it as one crucial part and then, please, keep listening.

If these aren't the part of trans life trans people themselves would like you to know, then how have these stories become so prevalent?

Because we, as trans people, are not the ones in control of the trans news story.

In 2014, American scholar Jamie Collette Capuzza published a study analysing sourcing patterns of trans stories in the US media. Looking at data from the preceding four years, Capuzza found evidence to support what has long been noted within our trans communities: trans people are far more likely to be written *about* as an 'issue' than we are to be recording our experiences and insights as equal participants. Just as often as not, the cis journalists writing an article or putting together a news segment would fail to include even a single quote from a trans person. Of the trans people who were quoted, the vast majority were white, the vast majority were trans women, and trans people who don't fit into the gender binary were hardly present at all.

Beyond that, Capuzza found a distinct skewering of focus: trans people were far more likely to be written and talked about in the entertainment, beauty and lifestyle sections of the media than in the 'hard news' categories of political, legal, economic and medical reporting.

Trans people are not always – not even often – approached by the press for comment or explanation when trans topics come up. When we are allowed to speak for ourselves, our answers are usually trimmed to fit a script written by others. And when that script is offered up as the truth of what trans people are, used as the foundation for future script writers, then we end up with a trans 'reality' created and maintained by those who aren't: a perfect trans chimera that mutates into the snake swallowing its own tail.

This isn't just a trans thing, of course; all kinds of people and subjects are distorted by reporting. The 'news' is a funny combination of playing to a known audience, keeping ad revenue on side, trying to attract attention in a crowded marketplace and appealing to the political sensibilities of editors and stakeholders. Sometimes there's some great journalism thrown in as well, if we're lucky. But when not all that many cis people know a trans person in real life – or don't think that they do – that understanding of the margin of difference between the media spin and the everyday reality can slip down to nothing at all.

We can be misinterpreted through lack of representation – but also through the particular prejudices of popular writers. The denial of reality, the cutting of a story to fit a particular narrative, and presenting uninformed opinion as fact: on a weekly basis, these are the ways in which trans people are represented to the wider world by those who know nothing about our lives.

What would someone who has never met a trans person – never worked alongside a trans colleague, had a beer with a trans friend, watched a movie with a trans sibling – think of Jeremy Clarkson's recent op-ed in *The Times*, 'Transgender Issues are Driving Me Nuts'? If you know Clarkson, you'll know that this is the kind of piece he made his fortune with: reactionary, cutting, the kind of thing described as 'not politically correct'. He writes: '[Children] dream impossible dreams. You don't actually take them seriously. You don't take them to a hospital when they're 10 and say, "He wants to be a girl, so can you lop his todger off?"' Anyone who knows anything about medical transition and the treatment of trans youth knows that genital reconstruction surgery is only available for adults. But those people are not who this article is written for – and the people for whom it *is* written now have another piece of proof that trans people are deranged, delusional and not to be trusted with children.

On a much subtler note is *New York* magazine's article on the removal of Kenneth Zucker from the Child Youth and Family Gender Identity Clinic in Toronto. A long-form read on the debate around the treatment of gender non-conforming children and teenagers, the reporting appears unbiased, nuanced – that suspect word, 'objective' – the kind of piece that requires time and attention from a reader, and rewards you for your efforts with the sense that you have learnt something concrete. But the article suffers from a number of omissions that would have given a more balanced picture of the current debate around treatment options for young people. Only a fraction of the research that contradicts Zucker's approach is mentioned: notable absences include an American Psychological Association award-winning paper from Y. Gavriel

Ansara and Peter Hegarty. The World Professional Association for Transgender Health, the global leader in standards of trans-related healthcare, has condemned reparative therapy – the kind of therapy Zucker is alleged to have practiced – as unethical. This vital detail is missing from *New York* magazine's article. The leading trans researcher consulted by the author on the historical, psychological and academic context for Zucker's work was not quoted, and more time is given to the trans activists who have protested Zucker's work than to the trans psychologists and researchers who have criticized his methods from within the field. The risk with articles such as this is that readers may be left with the impression that trans people are hypersensitive fanatics unable to function in the 'real world', most particularly that most logical of real worlds, that of scientific research and development. Researching the full detail of all the issues would take a full day and access to an academic library. It's heartbreaking.

And the most popular error of framing is, as ever, asking a non-expert to weigh in on a sensitive issue requiring expert knowledge. Before the publication of the results of the first-ever UK Trans Inquiry, a cross-party parliamentary investigation into the current state of trans rights and experiences in the UK, the *Evening Standard* published a piece entitled 'Changing Sex is Not to Be Done Just on a Whim'. Written with the kind of hyperbolic humour frequently found in newsprint editorials, the arguments contained within went beyond opinion and into the realm of misinformation. Following decades worth of campaigning from trans activists and extensive consultation from experts and laypeople from across the country, the inquiry recommended reforming the current confusing, time-consuming process of legal gender recognition, instead allowing UK trans people to update their documents with a simple online form. That update has already enjoyed great success in Ireland, with no sign of complications or dire societal fallout. But instead of focusing on these facts, and the genuine debate around them, the author instead weighed in against 'gender as a choice issue' and misrepresented the concerns of trans campaigners and our supporters as displaying 'a worrying indifference to a basic question of what makes us ourselves'. It is not a furious or hateful piece, but it mattered. The *Evening Standard*, given away free every evening throughout London, is impossible to escape. Its message carries. And that line – that trans people 'change sex on a whim' – was one that I had heard again and again in political discussions leading up to the publication of said inquiry. Despite its lack of foundation, it is used as an excuse by lawmakers, civil servants and politicians to reject calls for a simplified change of legal gender. Even when the person spouting it claims that they don't personally believe it, they put that phrase in the mouth of 'the public', 'the electorate', and use it as a reason why trans people cannot be allowed to have equal rights. And while I might have read four or five excellent takedowns of this piece, of that idea, online, I'd be willing to bet that the people who were already primed to believe that trans people are fickle and confused read only that piece – and agreed with it.

This is the reason why it's insufficient to respond with accusations of being 'offended', to say that anyone who disagrees with these pieces is not obliged to read them and can take their support elsewhere. Trans people may choose not to consume transphobic media; we have no choice about living in a world shaped by this misinformation.

A study from the University of Saskatchewan, in Canada, published in 2014, showed the real-world impact of such media. Looking at personally and culturally endorsed stereotypes of trans people and behaviours, the researchers found that, in the absence of real-life experience, cis people fell back on what they had learnt through the media. Overwhelmingly, what they had 'learnt' was that trans people are 'confused'. Respondents, relying on images of trans people in films, in the news, on TV, described trans women as wig-wearing caricatures of femininity, who most likely had no ambitions beyond looking pretty and finding stereotypical feminine employment and male approval. Trans men, on the other hand, probably wanted to pursue typically masculine careers and hobbies – working on an oil rig, playing team sports – but were let down by their smaller, weaker bodies and inability to be accepted by 'real' men. Some choice words used to describe trans people were 'odd', 'gross' and 'freaks'.

For all of these reasons, large numbers of trans people refuse to have anything to do with the mainstream media. We do have alternatives, after all. I'm a member of the first generation to have had internet access at home. Being able to research trans people, trans history, surgical options, was a lifeline for me, although it took some getting used to. Compared with how trans youth use the internet now, my experiences are already archaic. I still had to learn the language from the mainstream media, before I had enough information, and the courage, to enter those words into a Yahoo! search. What I found was limited to a handful of forums, a small list of books and an overwhelming amount of vitriol and anti-trans hate. For many teenagers now, mainstream media is no longer the first place they hear the words 'transgender'; they already have the entire trans world, or an approximation of it, at their fingertips. They can follow the real-time transitions of popular vloggers, swap advice and support on Tumblr, learn the theory and practice of social justice through reading blog posts and online articles and catalogue their own transitions on Instagram. For trans adults, too, all that we can't find in a newspaper, on TV, in a cinema, is available for us in the comfort of our own homes. I recently binge-watched *Her Story*, an Emmy-nominated web series created by trans and queer women, starring trans and queer women. I was in heaven just watching trans people – actual trans people like me and my friends, but with better outfits – navigating questions of friendship, love, societal pressures and internal doubts. I put my money in for the crowd funding of *Happy Birthday Marsha* – a movie about the history of the Stonewall riots that is everything Roland Emmerich's spectacular flop *Stonewall* was not. There are trans speakers on TED, funny but serious lists on Cracked and BuzzFeed, and a host of well-informed, well-researched bloggers and academics to follow. Complexity, nuance, a basic level of humanity: trans people speaking for ourselves.

The only problem is, is that the people we need to reach are not always – not even often – there with us. As much as we can assume that private internet access is universal, it is not. When we rely entirely on alternative media, we cut ourselves off from those who cannot afford to join us. Even with that access, there are hurdles to overcome. You need a magic word to get in – a search word, a recommendation, a click-through – *something* that will open up your media options from the traditional to the new. You also need the will to seek out something different, the need to find something better. What I have found, in outreach and consultation and most specifically in political work, is that the people who have the greatest power to impact on trans people's lives through legislation, employment, housing and environment are also the people most likely to accept traditional media portrayals of what trans people are, and not understand the need to look elsewhere for representation

So, as much as I would like to say 'enough' – to withdraw from the mainstream media altogether, as consumer, as spectacle and as participant – some of us stay. We stay in the hope that, if at least one of our quotes makes it into a finished piece, then that quote will change one mind. We offer an interview, knowing that it will be cut and edited in ways we would not like, because we think of a young person without internet access, who might just pick up a paper copy because it's there. We go on television, then try to protect ourselves from the inevitable abuse that follows, because we hope to be heard by the people who would never dream of watching an online news show produced by trans people. And we become complicit in the machine, knowing that if other people had not done the same for us, we would not be here today to keep the fight going.

But we can still expect more, work for more and ask for better.

2

'Call Me Caitlyn'

I do not know Caitlyn Jenner. I do not know anybody who knows Caitlyn Jenner, nor anyone who has worked with Caitlyn Jenner and, to be honest, Caitlyn Jenner does not take up a great deal of my time. I say this to ward off the inevitable questions, because being trans in a post-Caitlyn Jenner world is a little bit like being British and visiting small-town America: no, I do not know your cousin Gary who lives in Brighton, no, I do not drink tea every day at 4 p.m., I have never met the Queen, and I'm sorry but I don't miss Princess Diana.

Caitlyn Jenner might well be the most famous trans person in the world, but I don't know a single trans person who would call her a trans icon. I don't say this to be cruel, but because I am confused as to who gave her that title, and why.

Mey Rude, trans editor for online magazine *Autostraddle*, sums up everything I've heard from my own London-based community here:

Apart from being a big moment, this is also a pretty strange one. It's strange that a trans woman who, so far, hasn't done any work in the trans community has been crowned our queen. It's strange that a trans woman who is famous, rich, white and conservative, four things that do not describe most trans women, is now the face most cis people think of when they hear the word 'transgender.' It's weird that people are saying that a famous, rich, white, conservative and conventionally attractive trans woman is humanizing trans people to a whole new group of people. Why didn't Janet Mock or Laverne Cox do that for them? Why didn't CeCe McDonald? Why didn't Islan Nettles?'

But look at this phenomenon in a historical context and I guess it isn't so surprising. The Caitlyn Jenner story, the Caitlyn Jenner brand is, for all the newness, all the talk of being game-changing, following a path that has been trodden before. Christine Jorgensen, labelled the GI Joe turned blonde bombshell, hit the headlines in the early 1950s and stayed there for nearly twenty years. Born in New York in 1926, Jorgensen travelled to Denmark to pursue medical transition after a brief spell in the army. She left the States a 'shy, miserable person' – she returned to see her story on the front page of the *New York Daily News*. Coverage of her transition garnered more press attention than the news of the polio vaccine and, in her role as glamorous media darling, Jorgensen's fortune was made.

An examination of the trans success stories of the past seven decades, as measured by media celebration, attention and pay-out, reveals a well-established pattern of which Caitlyn Jenner is simply the most recent example.

The first ingredient is the 'can you believe it?' element. A dramatic shift from hyper masculine to hyper feminine, or vice versa, is more shocking, more titillating and makes for a better scoop. Even if this sudden change is at odds with the actual story – how the trans person in question experienced their growing self-knowledge and transition – it can be used as a frame and a guide. 'Before' and 'after' photos are necessary props, preferably as stereotypically masculine and feminine as possible.

Next comes the Cinderella moment. Nobody wants to hear about waiting years for a doctor's appointment, waiting to see what dose of hormones works best, trying to unpick gendered expectations, trying to make sense of a frequently hostile world. Instead, what works best is an almost overnight 'sex change'; not an ordinary life lived in stages and negotiated with compromises and setbacks, but a magical transformation, granted with the wave of a wand.

And finally, in this most popular trans media script, there is the focus on simplification and exceptionalism. Instead of focusing on trans communities, the most common and the most pressing issues faced by trans people, these stories focus on personal fulfilment and the desire to fit in. Transphobia is relegated to personal slights suffered, rather than a deeply entrenched, multi-faceted problem. The trans subject becomes one of the 'good' trans people: not angry, ground down and difficult, but seemingly eager to jump through the hoops set for them by the cis majority.

This is not a personal attack on Caitlyn Jenner. I don't know her. I know that she has raised money for trans causes, and that she has raised awareness of young trans people contemplating suicide. I know that we have very different ideas about what it is to be a woman or a man or any other gender. I know that her political choices are not my choices. I know that I don't know anything of her private life, her character, the struggles that she must bear, as we all bear our own struggles. I know that she is not my icon, and not my representative, though I wish her every happiness.

I know that this conversation is so much bigger than the public figure of Caitlyn Jenner.

And I know that this historical link – between Caitlyn Jenner and Christine Jorgensen – extends to the trans communities impacted by this double-edged sword of media success and successive waves of visibility. And that we have a chance to do things better the second time around.

I believe that the reason why so many trans people today feel ambivalent towards Caitlyn Jenner is because she is our Christine Jorgensen. And because, half a century later, the members of our community who are suffering the most are still being ignored in favour of a glamorous makeover and a tell-all story.

During the years when Christine Jorgensen was working on the movie adaption of her autobiography, there were many other trans people in the United States making waves of their own. Unlike Jorgensen, the media paid them little attention. Unlike Jorgensen, they didn't get compensated for their work. *The Christine Jorgensen Story* was proposed in 1960 and hit cinemas in 1970, complete with lurid marketing and the tagline: 'Did the surgeon's knife make me a woman or a freak?' For Jorgensen, just another aspect of the media machine; for those without her privileges, a life-or-death question, most often answered with hatred and violence. It was not a situation that could hold for long.

Nineteen sixty-five saw one of the first in a line of protests that would lead to the famous Stonewall riots, considered by many to be the birth of the LGBT movement we know today. Dewey's Lunch Counter in Philadelphia had been refusing to serve gender non-conforming customers: queer and trans people who didn't look the way society thought they should, who didn't act in a so-called appropriate manner. So those same customers – more than one hundred and fifty of them – turned up, sat down, and wouldn't leave. They handed out leaflets, and waited for the management to back down – which they did. The majority of the protesters at Dewey's Lunch Counter were black. They had taken some of the tactics from the civil rights movement, tried them in another setting – and won.

Another major protest followed the next year, at Compton's Cafeteria in San Francisco. In her groundbreaking 2008 work *Transgender History*, historian Susan Stryker recounts the details: that, again, it was the most vulnerable queer and trans people who came under attack, who were pushed too far, who fought back. What began with the usual police abuse finished in an all-out street fight. No date is available for the Compton's Cafeteria riot because recording it wasn't thought of as important: there was no press coverage, the police report disappeared, and when the surviving participants were interviewed, years later, they couldn't remember the exact day.

The reasons why it all kicked off are depressingly familiar to many trans people, and our wider communities, today: racism, classism, the pressures of gentrification, and the abuse of trans women by the police. Stryker explains:

The police could be especially vicious to 'street queens,' whom they considered bottom-of-the-barrel sex workers, and who were the least able to complain about mistreatment. Transgender women working the streets were often arrested on suspicion of prostitution even if they were just going to the corner store or talking to friends; they might be driven around in squad cars for hours, forced to perform oral sex, strip-searched, or, after arriving at the jail, humiliated in front of other prisoners. Transgender women in jail often would have their heads forcibly shaved, or if they resisted, be placed in solitary confinement in 'the hole'. And because they were legally men ... they would be placed in the men's jail, where their femininity made them especially vulnerable to sexual assault, rape, and murder.

The same people who paid money to gawk at Jorgensen, who might even call her 'brave', were all too often complicit in making and maintaining a world savage in its punishment of her trans siblings.

Which is not to say that this was Christine Jorgensen's fault, or that she did not do a great deal of good in the world – clearly, demonstrably, she did. She was a lifeline to hundreds of thousands of people, and her openness inspired compassion and hope in many. Her story, and her willingness to tell it, spread knowledge and spread ignorance, enlightened and erased. Both of these things can be true.

Of course, there are worse things than being ignored.

The last time I saw a trans woman on television – or, more correctly, the *character* of a trans woman on television – was during the latest series of *The X-Files*. I couldn't resist the pull of nostalgia, but wished I had with the introduction of 'Annabelle'. A minor background character, she appears only to flesh out the monster-of-the-week story. A black woman, a sex worker and, as is quickly explained, a trans woman who is also a drug addict. Who's had 'the surgery' – you know, on her genitals.

That's it. That's the joke. That's the reason for the character to exist: to be a black trans woman, who is a sex worker and a drug addict, because being that kind of woman, combining those particular traits, is apparently intrinsically funny. In a show designed to stretch credibility in all kinds of glorious ways, credibility disappears in an instant as Annabelle reveals her vulnerabilities to the FBI agents capable of arresting her and holding her in a men's prison – all for the sake of a punchline.

The inclusion of marginalised trans women as jokes or victims only is not a new trend. The long-running series *Crime Scene Investigation* has found a particular niche in sensationalising vulnerable trans women for ratings, offering us a psychotic trans murderer, numerous dead trans women (complete with genitalia jokes) and a 'delusional' trans woman stabbing herself to death.

Even an actress as gifted and groundbreaking as Laverne Cox has played these roles, early in her career. Before her breakthrough role in *Orange Is the New Black*, Cox appeared in *Law & Order*, *Law & Order: Special Victims Unit*, and in the role of 'Transsexual Prostitute' in *Bored to Death*.

As noted by *Bitch* magazine: 'In a 2012 survey, GLAAD found that transgender characters were victims in 40 percent of appearances. Additionally, 20 percent were sex workers. These are the roles people associate with transgender people, especially women.'

This is not about only wanting 'respectable' trans people to be portrayed.

This is about asking why these facts – that many trans people are sex workers, that many trans people turn to drugs and alcohol, that many trans people suffer violence both at the hands of those they know and at the hands of strangers, and that trans people who suffer from the effects of racism are most likely to suffer further violence and abuse – are suitable fodder for light entertainment, but not for an urgent and sincere investigation into the oppressions which are killing the most marginalised members of the trans community.

Instead of reporting on the *whys* of all of this – the scandals that are endemic racism, endemic transphobia, the particular hatred of trans femininity and womanhood that is trans-misogyny, the daily ways in which it is decided that some people are not as worthy of protection, of life, as others – instead, the lives of marginalised trans women are used as fodder for schlocky drama series, the background hum of an oversaturated media machine.

In the rare instances where real-life reporting does take place, the narrative tends to follow the fictionalised example. Scandal and titillation, the wrong names and the wrong pronouns, lurid accounts of violence committed and theories as to why (it's hinted) that violence could be justified. It can seem as though the journalists writing these reports forget the reality of what it is they're covering – very often the ending of a human life, the final, desperate moments of another human being – and instead write as though they're recapping an episode of the latest crime serial.

When leading human rights lawyer Sonia Burgess was pushed to her death on the London tube tracks in 2010, the mainstream media coverage was, in the opinion of many trans people and our supporters, depressingly lacking in sensitivity. Some reporters focused on unconnected and salacious details of the victim's sex life; most misgendered both the deceased and the accused, a fellow transgender person. Headlines such as 'Sex change "woman" accused of killing cross-dress lawyer on Tube' felt like a trivialization of a tragedy. The behaviour of the media was so upsetting that it led to the founding of All About Trans, a UK charity devoted to ending transphobia in the press.

Five years later, Senthooran/Nina Kanagasingham*, the person responsible for Sonia Burgess's death, was found dead in their police cell. They had suffocated to death with their hands bound and a plastic bag over their head – fellow prisoners reported hearing them shouting 'Help me' before their body was discovered. None of the newspapers that had so readily reported on Kanagasingham's appearance and demeanour when on trial could be bothered to record the result of the inquest into their death: 'self-inflicted', according to the National Offender Management Service Deaths in Custody Database.

And it's not only this exploitation of the suffering and deaths of the most marginalised trans people that does so much damage, but the ways in which it is *only* this suffering, these deaths, which are considered newsworthy. In all the trans-related media I've consumed, I could count on one hand the mainstream outlets that have covered the lives of marginalised trans people in an accurate and respectful way, rather than simply capitalising on their pain. A 'sensational' murder may be worth a headline, but nothing of the artists, lawyers, advocates, protesters, activists, everyday and extraordinary people resisting and fighting and thriving. The 2015 film *Tangerine*, following a day in the life of two trans women of colour, received widespread critical praise – but has nothing like the reach of a popular TV show or tabloid newspaper. There's a reason why so many trans people are such fans of prison dramedy *Orange Is the New Black*: where else do we get to see such a realistic, respectfully written trans character, beautifully portrayed by a trans actress, highlighting real issues faced by trans people? Activists who flip the script on who gets to be the subject of the news, who gets to write the story and what that story contains – women like Monica Jones, Miss Major and Lourdes Hunter – are rightly praised by online LGBT outlets, but I have yet to see their groundbreaking work covered by the mainstream press. There is a strict dichotomy of trans narratives which are deemed 'worthy' and those that are not. There is endless space available to speculate on whether Caitlyn Jenner will detransition, or to number trans women of colour as misnamed, misgendered victims of violent crime. For documenting the richness of the lives of those challenging this system? Not so much.

These are the two sides of the coin, the two ways in which trans people – overwhelmingly trans women – are portrayed. On one the glamorous 'sex change' and, on the other, the victim, the freak, the joke, the threat. For one, power (of a kind), and for the other, none.

And maybe this is why, after all, I do have something to say about Caitlyn Jenner. Because, despite her wealth, despite her whiteness, her prestige and her celebrity, huge numbers of people still laugh at her. They call her a man in social media memes, and journalists are paid to write op-eds in which they deny her the right to define her own gender. You can purchase a Caitlyn Jenner Hallowe'en costume, complete with basque and mask, and you can rip her apart in a comedy routine. You can make her pronouns conditional; watch those liberal 'shes' turn into 'hes' when she says something out of line. She is protected from the worst of what trans people go through, but the received truth of her gender is still predicated on the goodwill of the cis majority. The received truths of all our genders are too often predicated on the goodwill of the cis majority. One side of the coin is far safer than the other, but that safety is not guaranteed, and not often ours to secure. There is a spectrum of experience, of danger and prejudice to safety and success: Caitlyn Jenner is further along that spectrum than the majority of trans people, but cannot escape it. We are all still linked.

And this, then, is the reason why, despite not knowing Caitlyn Jenner, I can feel let down by her actions. Because one of the reasons for her popularity is that she's seemingly cool with this media narrative, seemingly okay with the assumptions and limitations – at least in public. Instead of using the advantage she has to tackle a hatred that hurts us all, she plays into the stereotypes, laughs along with the jokes, positions herself against the less palatable (more 'political') members of our community, and aligns herself with those who are doing the most to hurt us. One of the saddest things I've learnt, consulting with members of the mainstream media on trans coverage, is that there are plenty of cis people in the industry who don't like what they usually hear from trans activists: please stop hurting us, please stop misrepresenting us, please stop demeaning us. If Caitlyn Jenner says it's not that bad, then they would rather believe her. If Caitlyn Jenner's made it, why haven't you?

It is, perhaps, old-fashioned to believe in the idea of moral debt and moral duty. It's certainly not something I could impose upon anyone else, and I understand the opposition to it: why should Caitlyn Jenner be expected to do more for trans people, simply because she's trans herself? Why should trans people have to work harder, be less selfish, than everyone else? But when I think of how much has been given for so little reward by all the trans people before us – when I realise that neither I nor Caitlyn Jenner would exist as we are without the suffering and sacrifices of our shared communities – then I can't pretend that that debt isn't there, acknowledged or not.

I'll say it one more time – I don't know Caitlyn Jenner. I don't know if the insults hurled against her, the denial of her reality, hurt her – they would certainly hurt me. But the real-life implication of the attitudes she lets slide – that trans women are actually men, that the underlying issues of inequality and prejudice matter less than looking right and fitting in, that you can't expect cis people to do better – those attitudes feed the foundation of apathy, ignorance and cruelty that harms trans people without her protections.

Caitlyn Jenner is, most likely, the most powerful trans woman in the world. Think of what she could do, if she wanted to.

3

Finding My Voice

Before I learnt that there were words for people like me, I knew what it was I was looking for. I just didn't know how to capture that in a way I could fit into my world and hold onto, to put my feelings into language. Without language, those feelings couldn't solidify. Instead of a stable narrative, my memories of growing up to be what I could later call gender-queer are little flashes of recognition and fascination, sunk back down into what I had been taught I should be.

I spent a lot of time staring at famous faces in absolute wonder: Grace Jones, David Bowie, Lou Reed, Tracy Chapman, Brian Molko, Patti Smith. I had no idea what these people's genders were, but I knew that I couldn't tell by looking; that when I looked at them I felt full of pos-sibilities and longing. I felt the same way about expressions of androgyny in classical art, in movies, in poetry. Where I couldn't find them, I made them up; there were so many experiments with clothes and hair and makeup behind my bedroom door. I had murky, childish fantasies of being able to change my sex in any way I liked just by pressing a button on a magical machine. One of my most persistent daydreams was that, as an adult, nobody would be able to tell what my gender was, but that I would be so talented and so charming that nobody would ever try to find out.

But I can't overstate how hard it was to recognise myself as neither/nor when the whole world seemed to run as one or the other. There seemed to be a little gender leeway allowed for some kinds of gay people – for gay men who did drag and butch lesbians – but both of those categories made me feel like an outsider looking in. The model of transsexuality I'd heard whispers of was similarly fraught. 'Transsexual', in this definition, meant a man who wanted to be a woman, or a woman who wanted to be a man. In the ways in which they were discussed by others, these people were still trapped by other people's definitions, and the best they could hope for was to exchange one set for another, if they accepted being treated as a freak show. Beside which, there was the question of surety. In the newspapers, transsexual women always said 'I knew I was a girl', 'I was a woman trapped in the body of a man', but I barely knew what it felt like to be me, and didn't know how I was meant to decide whether that internal experience fitted into a boy or a girl camp. I felt trapped in my body a great deal of the time, but not all parts of my body: not my hands and not my voice. They always felt real to me. I could know that I needed my body to be different and, almost in the same moment, lose that knowledge from fear and from the impossibility of realising those differences in an honest way.

It came to a head when I came out. I wasn't sure of what I was meant to call my gender or do about my body, but I needed to be honest about my sexuality, so I told my friends, classmates, family, that I was bisexual (queer for preference), and then added the rejoinder 'gender blind', because it was the best term I could come up with on my own. I mostly settled on the androgynous style that made me feel most like myself, and the binding that paradoxically left me able to breathe, but still felt enormous pressure to present myself the way other people wanted me to be – to be found attractive.

People had commented on my gendered appearance and behaviour before: now, it was a subject for public debate. Some people said that they knew I had to be one way, because I was so 'forceful', 'dominant' and 'like a man'. There were as many saying that I had to be the other, and for the opposite reasons – femininity and prettiness. Girls excused their crushes on me by saying I was like a boy, and boys got angry with me for their crushes, because why couldn't I be more like a girl? All of that pressure pushed me into having to find an answer – but still I had no language.

After a year of reading absolutely everything I could find on being queer, I started noticing the breadcrumb trail left in the margins, in the footnotes. Alison Bechdel, author of *Dykes to Watch Out For*, was a godsend: the background detail of her comic strip often included the names of influential LGBT works and authors. I discovered Kate Bornstein, and ordered a copy of *My Gender Workbook* from America. I felt as nervous as if I had ordered porn through the mail. When it arrived, I could barely stand to open it, despite how desperate I was to learn what was inside. It was the old naming magic: I knew that, once I had the words, I wouldn't be able to escape the fact of what I was. Bornstein used the term 'transgender' and in her broad, evolving description – the contrasting descriptions of other trans people which she included alongside her own – I knew I had an answer. Not that I had a category I could slot myself into, but that I finally had the key to unlock all that I needed to tell about myself, and a tool with which to craft my future. I found a T-shirt that said 'gender free' and wore it with great pride, alongside my Doc Martens, black suits and heavy eyeliner. I grew up, went to university, grew up some more, got better at explaining myself, set my heart on medical transition, had my plans changed by bad luck, got there in the end, found my place. I'm sure I'll collect more words in the end, and look forward to watching them change and evolve in turn.

A question I am often asked is why, as someone who wants to subvert gender norms, I would want or need an additional gendered label. Couldn't I simply refuse all descriptors? Or, failing that, call myself a feminine man or a masculine woman?

What this question misses is the twofold job of words like transgender, genderqueer, genderfuck, androgynous. They do duty as the personal language for who I am but, far more importantly, their usage helps to develop a cultural language of greater gender plurality and nuance.

It's not about absolutes, or strict lines of demarcation between degrees of gendered expression. There are women in the world far more masculine than I am, and men far more feminine. I don't want to force them to use my words, and nor do I have a desire to steal theirs. This isn't about creating more fixed categories, with more rules about who can and can't be admitted.

It's about understanding that there needs to be space in

our shared cultural language for every individual iteration of selfhood to be communicated accurately. We find our own personal language within the broader terms, and accept the universality of the broader terms within our own personal experience.

What is right for me is my own use of transgender, androgynous, genderqueer. It is in my appearance, in my crafting of my sexed body, in how I see myself in the world; a denial of being either a man or a woman, and the embracing of many wonderful things in both of those categories. It is only a way to live outside of the gender binary: there are millions more. Some of these ways will seem obvious to an outsider, and some ways won't, but they are all of them valid, and each word used is worth learning. Every time each one of us uses these gendered words, and others, we are enriching the total meaning of every term. The more we expand our definitions, the more space there is for everyone.

We push for the inclusion of these words into our common lexicon because, without them, it is so much easier to pretend that we're too impossible to exist. Being genderqueer can be a daily fight against being made invisible. My words are a challenge to the people who would strip my experiences from me. What can be described can be communicated and made real, becomes a shield against that invisibility and dissolution.

Trying to take away someone's language is usually the first step in trying to change them. When I was twenty-one I worked as a volunteer at the London Lesbian and Gay Switchboard, a phone advice and listening service that was meant to serve the entire LGBT community. While explaining who I was, that I was transgender, one of the trainers shot me down; I couldn't be transgender, she said, because I didn't look transgender. Obviously, I was 'just' a drag king. That's what she wanted me to be, so that's what she described. My ordering of my experiences into my own descriptors is a challenge to that kind of erasure.

Pronouns are a vital case in point. I do not doubt that the recent surge in the visibility of people like me is linked to the increased use of the singular 'they' as a gender-neutral pronoun. When I was coming out, even that basic building block was lacking. Every time I was referred to with the wrong pronoun, a fundamental part of me was spoken away. The proposed pronouns I had read about – sie and hir – didn't translate into daily speech, at least not for the people around me. Now, through the use of they, I can feel the daily difference made by a language that supports the validity of my self. Each correct usage solidifies the awareness that people like me are just as much a part of the world as any other person.

Having found my own voice, my own language, was part of the battle. The other part, far from over, is in trying to be understood by other people not prepared to understand.

The majority of strangers still try to place me as male or female. On any given day, I'll collect a handful of gendered labels: 'sir', 'miss', 'madam', 'mate' and (my favourite) 'my good man'. In the face of disagreement, some people can double down on their need to enforce what they see. One time, ordering a coffee to go, I listened to two baristas argue over what to call me. They kept correcting each other's language: 'did she want a small or a regular?' 'No, *he* wanted a large, no cream'. I joke that the difference between being

a man or a woman is half an inch more on my undercut
but, genuinely, how other people decide me is frequently
confusing. I've been called sir with my mascara running,
and miss in a three-piece suit. Being a semi-public figure, I
find appraisals of myself in odd places; an academic text on
the meaning of gendered identities was the strangest. The
author was at pains to dissect my haircut along gendered
lines, describing the shaved back and sides as masculine, the
'shock' of hair in the front as feminine. If they had asked me,
I could have told them that the reason I've sported a standard issue hipster undercut for the past five years is because
I live in central London and I found the temptation too great
to resist. Once, in a masterclass, the famous singer giving
instruction to a room full of young musicians waved her hand
to encompass the whole of me and said, 'I don't know what
this is.' She couldn't even name me. I would be scattered
away into pieces if I let other people decide me in their own
words.

What the people who fail to understand me as I am
might be surprised to learn is that their way of reacting to
me, while common, is not the only way. Even when we are
confused about someone's gender, and don't have a greater
awareness of what it means to be trans, we have a choice to
respond with kindness rather than cruelty. I've had some
very special conversations with my nana about appearance,
gendered norms and being yourself; with her usual talent for
appropriate understatement, she says, 'Where would we be
if we were all the same?' I've had similar conversations with
my partner's grandmother over coffee after dinner, about the
gendered pressures we all feel, the compromises we all make
between who we want to be and how the world wants us to

behave. I teach music to students of all ages; I have never found a child who has a problem with how I look or how I refer to myself. Some older students can be – for want of a less anachronistic word – cheeky: one bright teenager who thought he could waste some lesson time by asking 'Why do you look like Justin Bieber?', and by calling me 'sir/miss/sir/miss/sir/miss/sir'. It was teasing, but it wasn't cruel. Younger children seem to accept what they see without worrying. One small student asked me, during our second lesson, 'Why do you look like a boy?' I told her it was because I liked looking like a boy, and asked her what she liked to look like. She thought for a second, and then said 'Tinkerbell'. After she had dusted herself with sparkly fairy powder we went back to learning about Middle C, confident in the knowledge that looking how you want to look makes you better at piano. I've had people of all ages use a 'they' pronoun to refer to me, without me asking them to, and I have friends and colleagues who had never met a trans person before they met me and yet took my gender, my pronouns, in their stride. It seems to have far less to do with gender than it does with broader issues of empathy and humility, and a willingness to understand that we are each the experts on our own lives.

I'm not sure how much longer it will take for people outside of the gender binary to be considered legitimate. The rate of change so far has taken me by surprise, both in our current race forward and in our longer, historical tendency to forget and roll back. What I am sure of, though, is that accepting people outside of the gender binary has less to do with the idea of specific non-binary genders, and a lot more to do with working away from binary thinking in general. That we get better at seeing beyond us and them, valid

and invalid, natural and unnatural, good and bad, and communicate instead the fullness of who we are to each other,
respectfully, with compassion. When we are surrounded by
such diversity – in nature, in culture, in human spirit – how
can we stand not to acknowledge it?

Not every – maybe even not many – people will want to
designate their own gendered experiences as being outside
of the binary. But working for a less binary world would not
only benefit trans people like me: we would all be the richer
for it.

4

Couldn't You Just . . . Not Be?

Like many children, I adored the Narnia books by C. S.
Lewis, and reread them constantly. The scene between
Susan, Peter and the Professor in *The Lion, The Witch and
the Wardrobe* always had a special resonance for me; it felt
like there was an important lesson to be learnt. Susan and
Peter have come to ask for advice on what to do about Lucy's
unbelievable stories of falling through the back of a wardrobe and finding a brand new world. The Professor, whom
we know to be extremely wise by his eccentricity and book-
filled study, considers this problem, and asks Susan and Peter
if Lucy is either mad or a liar. They all agree that it is clear
that she is neither. Well, says the Professor: 'You know she
doesn't tell lies and it is obvious that she is not mad. For the
moment then and unless any further evidence turns up, we
must assume that she is telling the truth.'

When I have to convince the sceptical of the truth of my
transness, I very often feel like Lucy.

It's amazing the number of people who'll try to argue other

41

people out of being trans, as if no one else has ever tried before. Sometimes those doing the arguing are motivated by concern, and sometimes by annoyance, confusion or outrage. Their 'arguments' are presented as rational undoings of our supposedly broken reasoning, as though being trans is a riddle which can be solved with the correct interpretation.

Perhaps even stranger are those people who present no arguments at all but who wonder, gently, if we've considered just ... not being trans. Just, maybe, avoiding it until it goes away. It often comes down to the split between words and deeds, the question: 'Well, why do you have to do anything about it?' I heard that one a lot when I first informed people of my intent to medically transition. I suspect it's the same kind of reasoning as the injunction to do as you like in private, but make sure you don't do it in the street and frighten the horses.

Underlying all of this is the idea that being trans is something unfortunate, impossible to understand and better to ignore. Something you could probably change, if you put your mind to it, or grow out of, if you'd just see sense. That can turn so easily from 'Why do you have to do this?' to 'Why are you like this in the first place?'

I don't have a quick and easy answer as to why I'm trans, no more than as to why I'm a pianist, or how I experience the colour blue. I don't have to know every *why* of who I am to know the truth of my existence, and know that I can only find happiness by embracing that truth. It doesn't make sense to me to try to reduce an enormous spectrum of human experiences to an on/off diagnostic, rather than following the more complicated and rewarding journey of investigating the totality of the human animal. But I feel the temptation to find a simple answer, when other people are so quick to provide their own reasons as to why I'm trans and – within those reasons – blueprints as to how I could change.

The most common explanations for my transness given to me by other people?

1. That I'm a freak of nature.
2. That I'm desperate for attention.
3. That I'm mentally ill.
4. That I *hate* nature, and want to go against it as some kind of rebellion.
5. That I hate women.
6. That I have unresolved issues with my mother.
7. That I'm scared to be a butch lesbian.
8. Because being trans is cool now.

The resolutions to all of these 'explanations' are alarmingly simple, and multifunctional: stop being mad, stop being difficult, stop pretending, stop existing.

Naturally, both the resolutions and the explanations fall far short of reality. I'm both an operatic and alternative singer; when it comes to attention I'd rather have the applause of an audience than transphobic insults in the street, and it's far easier to appear cool with the latest haircut than through coming out as trans. By virtue of being mentally ill and being in therapy for more than half my life, I'm confident that being trans is *not* a mental illness, and also of the fact that, if I somehow did hate women and not know it, my therapist would have told me and helped me work through it. I love my mother dearly but not in a Freudian way, and do not *fear* being a butch lesbian but, rather, acknowledge all the ways in which I do not fit that category. As for being a freak of nature, or desperate to deny its truth? I don't understand how being true to my nature goes against it. I can't begin to square that circle.

It is the question of surety that typifies this interrogative position most clearly for me. 'Are you sure?' is a constant refrain, the response given to my name, my passport, my pronouns, my title. It's the final question my surgeon asked me before I went under, and the first question friends of friends offered on hearing that I was going to have surgery.

Being trans is not like other aspects of life, where necessary elements of doubt are considered natural. Where there would otherwise be investigation, vacillation, self-doubt and fumbling – fear necessarily bound up with desire, belief with trepidation – there can only be flat, unquestioning stasis.

To be trans, you have to be surer than you've ever been, because being trans is what you are when you've exhausted every other option. And still, other people would like there to be a chance of something different, and so they ask 'Are you sure?', just in case.

To be accepted for transition-related medical care in the UK you usually have to pass the Real Life Test – a revealing title. The Real Life Test means living in your 'acquired gender' for a period of time, sometimes up to two years, without treatment, to make sure that you're really sure. Asking someone to go without the hormones they're desperate for, while also navigating the world in a body more likely to be read as non-normative, might seem cruel but, presumably, that is the point. You have to run the gauntlet to prove your worth. If you don't want it enough to expose yourself to violence, ridicule, the loss of employment, the loss of a home, then you don't want it enough to be sure. If, after a certain period of time, you'd like to update your birth certificate, and make sure that your legal documents are in order, then you need to apply to the governmental Gender Recognition Committee, a panel of anonymous strangers, who are there to decide if you're sure enough about who you are to be officially recognised in your own life. To them you must prove that you 'intend to live in the acquired gender until death' – they do not need to prove to you that they are worthy of making a judgement call about your surety. If your life has deviated in any way from the standard trans narrative you must provide explanatory evidence to back up your claim of being sure. If your claim is rejected, you cannot update your birth certificate, and cannot be fully classed as your own gender. You can try again, but each attempt will cost you.

Most trans people have our moments of surety, moments that vibrate with the rightness of knowledge through every part of us in sympathetic resonance. But we also know that those moments are to be feared, and to be denied, if possible. Those moments happen to other people, because trans people are not normal, and not like us, and how can we be harbouring that feared other inside ourselves?

We torment ourselves: 'How can I know for sure?' 'What if I'm wrong?' 'What would happen to me if I'm wrong?'

We hold off our transitions until it is transition or die. We are encouraged to do so.

And some of us die.

Many of us who live have tried to.

We could do this differently, if those who were so scared of us could learn to pick away at that fear. Transition can be another word for learning, or the inevitable transformation that comes as a foundation of living. It can exist in multiples. It can flow in many directions.

Some people are sure of being one gender all their lives. Some are sure for years, and then sure for another gender, another way of being. Sometimes transition is a way of being safe, and sometimes it's a way of daring to disrupt safety and play with chance.

With the confidence and comfort of more than a decade of living openly as myself, of being loved as myself no matter the hostility of the majority, surety matters less than it used to.

I am not sure that I will be the same for the rest of my life. I am not sure that my needs will remain static or that I will not seek further expression for an expanded and maturing self. I know myself, but not all that I could become, the good and the bad. What I am sure of is that there was no line I crossed that turned me from someone who could have been diverted into someone who was unquestionably trans. I think there are decisions I could have made differently, and choices I turned away from. If every point of departure splits into another world, I don't claim that every iteration would ultimately prove the same.

But I do believe that the only purpose served by the question of surety is to bolster the illusion that those who ask it have created: that they themselves are sure, and safe, and not in the slightest like us, the ones they are judging.

Even when you are sure you're sure, society can still try to make you disappear. It can call you a liar and a fraud and exclude you in all kinds of ways, large and small.

Bodily dysphoria, the sense that the felt sexed body is not right and needs alteration, is a burden that many, but not all, trans people bear. But there is another kind of dysphoria, one I have found common to every trans person I have ever met. Social dysphoria: the collision between who we are, how we should be, how we need to express ourselves and live our lives, and the gendered straitjackets others would force us into. It is the misery, the wrongness, of being forced to live a lie. The pain of being called fakes for our authenticity.

It is being turned invisible, which serves a dual role; not only is our disquieting presence removed, but the pain we experience as a result can be safely ignored.

Some critics of trans people have told us that we shouldn't feel this pain at being denied the legitimacy of our own selves; gender is, of course, just a social construct.

I wonder if these people also tell widows not to bother grieving over their husbands, because marriage is also just another social construct. Love, justice, mercy, faith: all just social constructs. It's a nonsensical argument that understands nothing of how we are constructed as social creatures, how we have created our interlocking but individual worlds of being human. Trying to deny us the right to exist as we know we are is to deny us the right to exist.

The results of that pressure? To stop being? Two of the biggest surveys ever carried out on trans populations can give us part of the answer. Based in the USA and the EU respectively, what they have found chimes with research data, and community-based evidence, from around the world. The first, from 2011, was carried out by the National Center for Transgender Equality in the USA; this is their summation of their findings:

Transgender and gender non-conforming people face injustice at every turn: in childhood homes, in school systems that promise to shelter and educate, in harsh and exclusionary workplaces, at the grocery store, the hotel front desk, in doctors' offices and emergency rooms, before judges and at the hands of landlords, police officers, health care workers and other service providers.

This report is a litany of suffering. A full 41 per cent of respondents had attempted suicide, compared with 1.6 per cent of the general population. Seventy-eight per cent of gender non-conforming kids had experienced harassment at school; 15 per cent were forced to leave school to escape abuse. Nearly half of all respondents had been discriminated against in employment, which makes sense of the fact that 16 per cent of respondents worked in underground economies as a way to survive. Around one-fifth had experienced homelessness as a direct result of being trans, and the majority of those who sought shelter at a refuge were further harassed, assaulted, or simply turned away. More than half of respondents had been harassed in a public place; more than a quarter had been harassed by police. More than a quarter of respondents reported being abused in a medical setting: being mocked by staff after suicide attempts, undressed and left on public display, forced into unnecessary genital exams. Across the board, people of colour suffered more than white people; racism and transphobia is a terrifying combination.

A similar survey was produced by the European Union Agency for Fundamental Rights in 2014. With 6,569 respondents, it is the largest study yet of trans people, and found that: 'the survey results depict a disturbing reality. They show that the equality of trans persons is, as yet, a hard-to-reach goal.' The results are strikingly similar to the American study. More than half of respondents had been personally discriminated against for being trans, and more than a quarter of trans students experienced *frequent* harassment in school. One in five respondents were discriminated against in health care and social services, and the same number were discriminated against when trying to find a place to live. Many had been the victims of hate crimes, but most did not reports those crimes to the police, believing both that the police would not want to help and also that the police themselves are a source of danger. The more open a person was about being trans, the more likely they were to be the victims of hatred, abuse and violence.

When you've suffered from the impact of other people's hatred, ignorance, callousness, it isn't just those instances that cause the damage: it's the long-term effect of each individual action, stacked up against each other. It's the cumulative impact of loss after loss: the loss of a job, the loss of a home, the loss of a family. It's the drip-drip-drip effect of bearing the weight of others' cruelties, and the means with which they alter the way you approach the world, and yourself. You lose the ability to trust in others, to trust in the future, to trust your own judgement. The walls close in; where do you find the strength to push back against them? It's so easy, from the outside, to say, 'I wouldn't let it get to me. I wouldn't care if other people didn't approve'. It's harder to feel that way when you know that the next person who doesn't approve might be the next person to assault you in the street, that the next person who doesn't understand will be the one standing between you and the job you need to keep going.

All of the research that I've seen – *all of it* – shows a global epidemic of stigmatisation, discrimination, erasure and violence against trans people. It astounds me that, in the face of all of this horror, so many of us are able to keep going, not just for ourselves, but for our shared communities, for each other. It is a tremendous testament to all those who've made it, despite the odds, but never an indictment of those no longer here. It is proof of the necessity of living an honest life.

We are not asking for pity when we describe the ways in which we are delegitimised and punished. We are asking for outrage, and respect for the fact that, despite all of this, we struggle on, and find joy as well as sadness. We are demonstrating our courage, and asking for shared strength.

What changes would we see, then, if cis people stopped calling us mad, and saw instead the insanity of a world that persisted in punishing us simply for telling the truth? What would we do with the knowledge of the reality of trans lives?

Until now, in the West, we have taken three main approaches to solving the problem of trans existence: ignore it, try to change it or support it. That last has been the rarest. Only one course, so far, has been proven to work.

Not all trans people will want or need medical treatment, but the ways in which trans people can (and cannot) access medical care can show in the particular what holds true in the universal. What is held up as the quintessential trans experience provides the starkest example of how we are written away.

Trying to ignore the fact of being trans is the most common option, and the one that nearly all trans people themselves have tried. It's the one we've been raised to, after all. We can ignore from fear, from the knowledge that who we really are would hurt the ones we love, out of a desire to avoid bigotry and censure, and because we have internalised every awful aspect of transphobia our culture has to offer.

When the need finally becomes too great, and we cannot ignore ourselves any longer, we can gather our courage and confide in the medical system where, too often, we are ignored all over again.

I took an option unavailable to the majority of trans people, and paid for my own treatment privately. Everything I had found out about the NHS gender treatment pathway told me that, in the late 2000s, I would not be offered care as an openly genderqueer person. My musical career meant that I couldn't follow the standard pathway of hormones followed by surgery and, after having had to delay surgery for many years to care for my brother when he became ill, I didn't know if I could wait any longer to try to fight for care I might never receive. I remembered the ways in which my ongoing mental health care had been cut off, and the pressure I had been under from doctors who did not know me to come off the antidepressants prescribed to me by my psychiatrist, because a young person on antidepressants did not fit their world view. Having experienced that kind of medical failure in one field, I wasn't prepared to try it in another. I used my savings, made the changes I needed, and learnt what it was to feel comfortable in my own skin. That basic and extraordinary freedom – of finally feeling at peace in my own body – available only because of the luck and privilege of being middle class with money in the bank.

This choice – pay for it yourself or go without – is common

to the majority of trans people who seek medical care. Globally, society has been slow to acknowledge the validity and necessity of these treatments. A few insurance plans will cover some transition-related care, and a few large corporations – hardly an option for the majority of trans people. Few nations, internationally speaking, fund hormonal, surgical and ancillary treatments for trans people. In countries like Britain, where a basic level of care is provided, the waiting lists can seem endless, and whether a trans person is allowed access to care is often at the mercy of individual doctors. We swap war stories via email lists, conferences and community meetings: GPs who withhold all care out of prejudice and spite, specialists who ask perverse questions, guidelines that place arbitrary and insulting demands on potential patients, waiting lists that last for years and drive many to desperation. Only a person who has never experienced the savage pain of bodily dysphoria, who refuses to listen to those who do, could think this an acceptable situation.

Placed in this impossible position, many people self-medicate: I know that I would. My personal experience with trans communities in the UK, Europe, North America and Australasia suggests that self-medication is extremely common, particularly now that hormones can be ordered online. Research projects into the health and wellbeing of trans people in India, Colombia and the Philippines have found that self-medication is the norm and, deprived of affordable surgical options, trans women will resort to self-surgery and peer-administered silicon injections. While dangerous, this is nothing new; sexologists in the early twentieth century found that European trans people were carrying out their own improvised genital surgeries, and injecting paraffin into their breasts to make them larger. Desperate people will do what they need to do. It's better than suicide – and that is something that happens, too.

Conversion, or aversion therapies, historically the second most popular way to deal with the 'trans problem', categorically and empathically do not work, though it's not for lack of trying. Sometimes trans people have been the ones to push for any chance to change, but more often conversion or aversion therapy has been forced on trans patients by parents, spouses and the state. Forced institutionalisation, forced drugging, electro-shock therapy, nausea-aversion therapy, shame-based 'solutions' – the twentieth and twenty-first centuries have seen variations on all of these methods, and what they have produced is not a cavalcade of newly minted cis people, but trans people who must live with the additional trauma of frequently violent and sometimes nonconsensual medicalisation. The pushback against these treatments is not new either. Michael Dillon, a British doctor and trans man, published *Self: A Study in Ethics and Endocrinology* in 1946. Speaking from experience, both clinical and personal, he argued that trans people could not be changed through therapy, and that the best course of treatment was to provide the hormones and surgeries that trans patients requested. Seventy years on, we are still fighting those who would go against a tidal wave of evidence because they have a personal problem with trans existence.

As many trans people have noted, it's baffling that some doctors, some laypeople, persist in thinking that trans people can be forced or shamed, convinced or persuaded out of being trans, when that is the same trick that society at large has been trying on us our entire lives, to no avail.

It's hard to think of a worse punishment for being trans than the punishments society so regularly metes out – physical violence, threats of violence, verbal abuse, emotional suffering – and yet here we are. Surely that tenacity must count for something.

I don't want to fall into saying, 'It's not my choice, I can't help it.' How can I pick myself apart and say 'Here is how I would be, if I weren't trans?' – it's a pointless, endless exercise. Neither do I want to play the game of 'But if I could be cis, would I?' What I will say is that when the world saw me as a certain kind of cis person, playing mostly by gendered rules and bending the more flexible ones, I was treated so much better than I am now. Society can sometimes be very obvious about punishment and reward, and seeming to be a cis person guaranteed not just the absence of punishment, but the active presence of reward. It didn't stop the misogyny, of course, but neither did transition. The kind of misogyny I experience is different, but it's roughly the same amount. What that false, cis reading of me did provide was all the little social kindnesses and steps up that make life so much easier: the smiles, the metaphorical doors held open, the preferential treatment, the attention and the praise. Being seen as a beautiful girl, a white girl, a thin able-bodied white girl with money and most of the symptoms of my mental illness temporarily hidden; society approved, and it let me know it. In that intersection of cisness and societal privilege I was taught what it was to be valued, even as sexism took its toll. Far better than any therapeutic ploy, the world around me taught me how it expected me to behave, how easy or how hard it could make my life. And it still didn't work.

But for those researchers and commentators who do not want to believe these facts, there is a final line of argument: that the treatments, social and medical, on offer to assist trans people simply do not work. It's a line still pulled by talking-head pundits and some doctors: they feel for us, but say that transition is a road to failure, and only conversion will help us find peace.

Inevitably, this claim is the product of ignorance and, sometimes, research now widely considered out of date and erroneous. A 1979 paper from Johns Hopkins University is the foundation point for the argument that physical transition is pointless, concluding that trans patients cannot be helped through medical means. Historian and sexologist Vern L. Bullough describes the flaws in Meyer and Reter's paper thus: 'The study was based upon 100 patients, thirty-four of whom had been operated on and sixty-six who had not. Twenty-four of the thirty-four had their surgery at Hopkins and ten had gone elsewhere. The sixty-six who had not been initially evaluated had either been denied surgery or changed their minds or went elsewhere. Only fifty percent of the total sample could be located, almost all of who had the surgery at Johns Hopkins but not many of the others. Still the study concluded that those who had the surgery did not have any better psychological adjustments than those who did not. Though it is clear that Meyer's and Reter's research was fraught with so many methodological flaws (including self-selected samples, no real measure of adjustment, and poor response rate) that many peer review journals would have rejected it, it did receive publication in part because there had been so few long term follow up studies (Fleming et al., 1980, Docter, 1988, and Money, 1991).' Critiques of this work, and further studies that demonstrated far more positive outcomes for trans patients, swiftly emerged.

Luckily, more than three decades of further academic research has given us a wealth of new data far more important than a simple critique of the old. It would be impossible to do justice to it all in this limited space; study after study after study has shown how trans people's lives improve when our need for physical transition is met with support rather than resistance. Those looking for more information would find a good starting point in the bibliography downloadable from the World Professional Association for Transgender Health website. Those looking to know how it feels, to have a chance at life in a congruent body, free of dysphoria? Just listen to trans people and what we know of our own lives. We have been speaking this truth for a long time.

Physical intervention – whether surgical, hormonal, life-style based or a combination of the three – should never be treated as a necessary component of being trans, nor should we adopt a one-size-fits-all policy. It was necessary for me, but in a way that did not follow the 'standard' route; every trans person will have their own, unique needs. For me, it becomes an issue of personal alignment, of revealing the body already felt to be there. It doesn't solve the problems of being trans in a transphobic world, but it can at least make our personal worlds right.

There is always the question of regret. I have chosen to answer this question last, because I am so tired of it coming front and centre whenever medical transition is discussed.

Yes, there are cases of regret. There are people who detransition. These cases are few and far between – the percentages are very small – but that doesn't mean they should be dismissed. With apologies to my friends who have detransitioned or retransitioned if I get this wrong, this is what I've learnt.

Some people who are counted under cases of 'regret' do not regret their treatment at all, but simply needed to pursue some further treatment to complete their transition. This is often the case for people who do not fit comfortably within the gender binary, as the treatment pathways available rarely offer support and options for people who may desire a mix of sexed traits. Other trans people who have expressed regret in the medical and community literature feel regret not over transitioning, but regret in their choice of surgeon and the results of their surgery. Some surgeons are excellent, but I know of several who have treated their trans patients badly, both in terms of results and in follow-up care. It doesn't surprise me that a trans person who cannot have a fistula repaired, for example, would regret choosing the surgeon who refuses to fix the results of their work. Some trans people who currently express regret will later go on to try transitioning again; it is a well-known occurrence for a trans person to need to try several times before they have the wherewithal to carry through their transition. It's not often easy. Family, friends and broader communities can exert a tremendous amount of pressure on a newly out trans person; 'regret' can often prove an initial withdrawal in the face of overwhelming disapproval.

And, finally, I do know a very small number of people who have detransitioned because they no longer feel like they are trans. One person explained it to me like this: sometimes life only presents you with short-term choices, and you have to take the choice that will get you through. You have to survive to have the benefit of hindsight. Transitioning got them through to a better place and, in that place, they could see that transition wasn't their final destination after all.

I don't believe that there should be any shame attached to taking a choice that was right at the moment of choosing, and then living to decide that, actually, another choice would be better. I think we should all be more open to the courage it takes to make both of those decisions.

Life is about risk. Every choice we make has the capacity to make our lives better or worse, to hurt or help us and the ones we love, to come to be something we regret or celebrate. We give our informed consent. I don't see why we should expect anything else, as trans people hoping for the basic right to breathe freely in our own bodies.

5

What About Sex?

It's surprisingly hard to find one standard, unified, non-contentious definition of what sex and gender actually *are*, and where the dividing line between the two lies. Does the truth of sex reside in the genitals, the hormones or somewhere deeper? Is gender an expression or subcategory of sex, a class system imposed by the patriarchy, a system of societal encoding, personal expression, all of the above? Sex and gender are totally separate: gender is a lie, sex is real: sex is gendered and also a lie. Some writers argue that 'female' and 'male' refer only to sex, 'man' and 'woman' only to gender, while others claim the reverse. This proliferation of terms and meanings matters on far more than a semantic level. Not only does it highlight one of the main stumbling blocks towards trans acceptance so far: it illuminates a different path towards that goal.

When it comes to sex, trans people are often told to stay in our lane. As the truism goes, sex is between your legs and gender is between your ears. We may assert the right to our gender 'identities'; we may even, if we are lucky, be accepted in those social roles. But, as I am frequently told, we shouldn't forget that those identities are surface-level, distinct from our 'biological sex' (male or female only); woe betide the person who might seek to confuse the issue. As absolute as the Cartesian dualism of mind and body, gender is a form of expression that can alter with culture, but sex is the fact of the body, and the body is unalterable – at least deep down, where it counts.

This is the understanding of the difference between 'sex' and 'gender' that I grew up with, and was taught to accept as fact. By this reasoning, a trans man might call himself a 'man', but still be labelled 'female', and vice versa for a trans woman. A genderqueer person like myself, no matter what changes they had made to their sexed body, would still be classed as the sex they were assigned at birth.

Whenever I come across someone suspicious of trans people and disinclined to believe us, I know, with a sinking certainty, that they will bring up the subject of chromosomes. It's the trump card, the incontrovertible factoid to rely on when confronted with an unknown or ambiguous presence. 'You can mutilate your body all you like – but you'll never change your chromosomes! You're XX/XY and that means female/male, and that's science. That's what you *really* are.' Science (note the capital 'S') has not found a reason for trans people to exist and, therefore, trans people cannot be real. As the movement for trans rights moves into the mainstream, and with it a growing awareness of gender diversity and plurality, the more I hear these statements used – often aggressively, often in desperation.

After more than a decade of learning, of experiencing life at the margins of sex and gender, I no longer believe this strict gender/sex divide to be true. Gender and sex can, and do, mean different things in different contexts. More than that, they interact. Why is it that we classify bodies into 'male' and 'female' first, rather than through any other categorisation? Why do so many ideas about sex cleave so strongly to gender stereotypes? Is it possible to consider the body as something neutral that exists apart from the sexed and gendered terms we use to describe it?

Some trans people would prefer to avoid the argument altogether, others to bring it to a head. I stand with the latter option. Not because trans people are a problem to be explained away – validated or refuted by a singular notion of scientific truth – but because, when the facts of our supposed sexes are used to invalidate and endanger us, it is too dangerous not to. Not only that: that the possibilities as to what trans people can teach us all about the science of sex and gender are too precious to dismiss.

*

If the state and the legal system have an interest in maintaining a two-party sexual system, they are in defiance of nature. For biologically speaking, there are many gradations running from female to male; and depending on how one calls the shots, one can argue that along that spectrum lie at least five sexes – and perhaps even more. For some time medical investigators have recognized the concept of the intersexual body ... Indeed, I would argue further that sex is a vast, infinitely malleable continuum that defies the constraints of even five categories.

So wrote pioneering biologist Anne Fausto-Sterling in her 1993 paper 'The Five Sexes: Why Male and Female Are

Not Enough'. In the twenty-plus years since its publication, we have been inundated by developments in the field of sex research, developments which complicate, broaden and enliven the old idea of a sex binary. Unlike the 'facts' most of us were taught at school – that there are two sexes, male and female, opposite versions of each other with discrete, non-overlapping traits – this new knowledge paints a far more detailed, nuanced picture of what sex *is*.

From the very first our idea of oppositional binary sex is undermined by two simple truths: that we are all formed from the same material, and that there are more than two patterns for our potential shaping. Not only are 'male' and 'female' far more similar than they are different, but there are many ways in which these themes can be combined and developed. This is no two-part invention, but a full-blown symphony. Rather than possessing distinct genital differences from the get-go, we all begin with a base potentiality: the urogenital swellings and phallus of early fetal development. The legacy of this mutual foundation can be seen in the shared similarities of the penile-clitoral area, for one example, or in the fusing of original tissue that leaves behind the penile raphe, the raised line running along the underside of the penis. Changing hormone levels in adulthood cause growth or shrinkage of the penis/clitoris and shifts in the strength, length and frequency of erection. That our bodies are capable of sexual reproduction is, arguably, an evolutionary advantage, but it doesn't make our sexed bodies opposites, and neither does it limit the possibilities of those bodies.

For many people, sexed development cannot be described in traditional 'female' or 'male' terms at all. Thanks to tireless work by activists, advocates and researchers, we now know that the number of intersex people (or people with diverse sex development) is far greater than previously thought. The exact number of people counted as intersex depends upon which physical variations are included in the count, and also on the cultural pressure to normalise genital diversity as 'malformation'. However, according to academic and activist Cary Gabriel Costello, if we acknowledge the many ways in which the body develops along intermediate lines (such as clitoromegaly and micropenis), as well as chromosomal and hormonal variations such as congenital adrenal hyperplasia and androgen insensitivity syndrome, then up to one in one hundred and fifty people could be described as intersex: 'about on par with the likelihood of having green eyes'.

So does this mean that trans people are a third (or fourth, or fifth?) sex? Is intersex another word for trans?

No. Intersex people and trans people face a multitude of different challenges, and there is a shameful history of trans people needing to pretend to be intersex to access medical care, in the hope that the medical establishment would consider their needs more valid. And yet, when considering what it is we know about sex, when exploring how the science of sex affects and is affected by gender, it is vital that intersex experiences are included. The existence of sexes beyond a simple male/female binary, and the experiences of people who have been punished for falling outside of those bounds, show us both how our cultural understanding of what sex is warps the evidence of nature and, through resistance and solidarity, shows us a better way of respecting all human bodies. Whether we are born with bodies that defy conventional male/female classification, or adapt those bodies later in life, we are better served by an idea of a sexual continuum than by the prison of two separate and opposite categories.

Intersex people, just like non-intersex people, are most likely to be women and men, the genders they were assigned at birth. Other intersex people would not describe themselves in binary terms, but neither would they place their experiences under the trans umbrella. With that said, it is also true that a not insignificant number of intersex people are also trans. When it comes to transition-related care, these intersex trans people are usually doubly discriminated against – often by doctors and sometimes, as in the UK, through legislation. In our sometimes different, sometimes linked struggles, we often face the same enemies.

Perhaps no greater proof of the fragility and toxicity of the binary myth exists than in the medical treatment of people with intersex traits. Now, and even more so in the past, surgeons have been quick to 'correct' the genitals of infants and children through surgery – invasive surgery on minors incapable of giving consent – in order to maintain the lie that only two forms of sexual development are possible. This practice is considered by many to amount to medical abuse. It was only in 2015 that Malta became the first country in the world to outlaw such interventions; this form of medical malpractice is a global problem, despite the condemnation of the World Health Organization and the UN Office of the High Commissioner for Human Rights. The scars – both emotional and physical – borne by the intersex people operated on can last a lifetime. It is staggering that such harm can be inflicted, and be so normalised, for the sake of maintaining a status quo. It is heartbreaking that bodily integrity, the sanctity of selfhood and the right to live free from pain could mean so little compared with the pressure to fit into a false dichotomy.

Trans or cis, intersex or not, we need to wake up to the fact that treating sex as a fixed and oppositional binary is not only a distortion of reality, but is doing active, extreme harm to a significant percentage of our population. Rather than forcibly applying a fantasy, to our very real detriment, we could decide to accept the reality, and learn and grow from there.

So, with that knowledge: if sex is not simply the division between two opposites, then what is it? For many researchers, the answer lies not in a static idea of what sex is, but in *how* the body can be sexed, in different ways and at different times.

Instead of talking about 'biological sex' as one uniform category, we can recognise the different components of our biological make-up, and recognise also the permutations that can exist within and between each one of these groupings.

We can think of sex as being expressed through six broad categories, each existing on a spectrum, capable of being combined in different ways. Chromosomes, hormones, internal sex organs, external sex organs, secondary sexual characteristics and general morphology: these are the aspects of our bodies that are affected by our potential for sexual reproduction. None are a simple either/or, but all contain room for variations. For most people these categories will align in a way we are taught to consider normal. We expect a man, for example, to have XY chromosomes, higher androgen levels and a standard processing of those androgens, testes and a prostate, a penis and scrotum, higher levels of body and facial hair and a broader, taller, more muscular body – and vice versa for women. But, while more common, these more typical alignments are no more valid than other combinations. The body of a trans women who has pursued hormone therapy and surgery might combine XY chromosomes, higher levels of oestrogen and progesterone with concurrent lower levels of/lower sensitivity to androgens, no testes, a prostate, a vulva and vagina, little body hair, no facial hair, breasts and curves. When looking at all the different parts of her physical make-up, what counts as 'biological sex'? All of these categories are sexed, and all are 'biological'. Why would any one category – chromosomes, for example – be given precedence over another? And why should it be a problem if some bodies combine a mix of traits?

The history of 'sex' chromosomes is fascinating for precisely this reason. Historian and philosopher of science Sarah Richardson charts this highly political history in her 2013 book, *Sex Itself: The Search for Male and Female in the Human Genome.* In a world increasingly confused by the challenges of sex and gender diversity, and faced with the ambiguities present in other sexed categories, early researchers jumped at the chance to label X and Y chromosomes the final, irrefutable proof of binary sex, investing in them a host of gendered stereotypes. The only problem is, as explained by science writer Ian Steadman, the fact that 'there are extremely few sexual characteristics solely controlled by the presence or absence of a Y chromosome – and just as there are plenty of characteristics controlled by genes found on other chromosomes, the 'sex' chromosomes also carry genes that determine traits that have nothing to do with sex. Y is not the essence of masculinity, nor is X that of femininity.'

In every sexed category what popular wisdom supposes it knows is a far cry from the diverse riches found in nature. Another favourite of the binary sex brigade is the idea of sex being 'hard-wired' in the brain as 'male' or 'female'. Academic psychologist Cordelia Fine's 2011 book *Delusions of Gender* – an essential work – analyses the supposed science behind the popular headlines. What she found makes for profoundly uncomfortable reading. Flawed methodology of all kinds, tiny sample sizes, incorrect forms of analysis, guesswork and unexamined bias; the studies and conclusions trotted out to provide proof of essential sexed differences veer strongly into the realm of 'neurofallacies', to use Fine's term. 'Male and female brains are of course far more similar than they are different. Not only is there generally great overlap in "male" and "female" patterns, but also, the male brain is like nothing in the world so much as a female brain. Neuroscientists can't even tell them apart at the individual level. So why focus on difference?'

That we are all shaped by the fact that we are creatures potentially capable of sexual reproduction is not in doubt. But all of us, trans or not, intersex or not, could stand to question the idea that this potentiality limits the possibilities of who we are and who we can be – and what we can be to each other.

The term 'sex change' has fallen out of favour over recent years, for a number of reasons. It's a crude phrase, one that reduces the totality of being trans to our sexed bodies, inviting questions about our most private parts. For the trans people who do seek medical intervention, the process is never as swift and simple as 'sex change' would imply.

Much as I've fantasised about swapping my body for one with a better fit, like exchanging a sweater one size too big, the actual process of transition is far less immediate, more akin to the cumulative changes of puberty than an extreme makeover.

But 'sex change' does manage to hint at an important truth frequently dismissed: that all of us will experience changes to our sexed characteristics over the course of a lifetime. Trans people might well experience the most obvious of these changes, but the process of change is common to us all.

One of the saddest bits of transphobia I've seen recently has been an online meme discussing trans women's breasts. The authors, trying to find a reason to support their claim that trans women's bodies are not 'natural', hit on this explanation: trans women are only able to grow breasts because of a change in hormone levels, so those breasts don't count as 'real'. How to distinguish between 'natural' and 'unnatural' changes to hormone levels was, sadly, not explained, nor how they believed that 'real' breasts came into being.

The same hormones that are administered to cis people for health reasons – to correct an imbalance, or as birth control – do not suddenly become fake when prescribed to trans patients. The changes we make to our secondary sexual characteristics, the shape and presentation of our bodies, are not 'deceptive'; these are our real bodies, self-declared, autonomously controlled. Surgical intervention might well be considered unnatural, but only insofar as all surgery could be named so. My voice, my throat, is not considered fraudulent because of the removal of my tonsils, and no one has ever called me unnatural because of the metal pinning together my right wrist. As with many other things labelled 'unnatural' by our society, a better explanation of that particular usage would be 'something I do not approve of'. Anal sex, being trans, pursuing IVF treatment, using condoms are all 'unnatural'. It is rarer to hear someone complain about the unnatural nature of chemotherapy, antibiotics or painkillers.

So many of us want the definition and meaning of sex to be safe, unchanging and foundational. When so much of our society is invested in maintaining the idea of sexual difference, it can be threatening to realise just how mutable those differences can be. And yet we cannot work for trans inclusion and acceptance if we cannot allow the inclusion of trans bodies into the spectrum of other acceptable sex changes. We celebrate other life-changing, life-giving medical developments in the field of sex research and medicine – why should trans-related changes be excluded from that celebration?

Puberty, pregnancy, childbirth, menopause: while these moments of change are frequently obscured by all manner of misinformation and culturally specific myth, we are all well aware of the seismic changes to our sexed bodies that occur over the course of a lifetime. Our genitals grow and develop, our secondary sexual characteristics mutate, illness or accident can mean the removal or modification of our reproductive organs. Our sexed bodies at seventy are not the same as our sexed bodies at seven: sex changes are a natural and necessary part of life. Even our chromosomes, the supposedly immutable touchstone of our sexed selves, are subject to change. Two thousand and twelve research at the University of Washington found something surprising in the brains of female test subjects: XY chromosomes. These women had experienced the phenomenon of microchimerism – the migration of stem cells between parent and child via the placenta. We don't yet know what effects, if any, these migrated cells might have; what is clear is that we have a lot more to learn.

Confusion over how bodies can change during transition is one factor in labelling trans bodies as unnatural. What, in reality, is a range of treatments that work to realign the body along slightly different lines – shaping what's there into a different variation of the same material – is often misrepresented as mutilation or quackery. But, when that confusion is cleared up, why would the sex changes of transition be counted in a separate category to the universal sex changes of life?

Hormonal, chromosomal, internal, genital, secondary sexual, morphological: six ways of categorising sexual development and difference.

What if we were to listen to trans people, and add a seventh?

'Trapped in the wrong body' is the cliché used to refer to bodily dysphoria inevitably trotted out by the mainstream media, and subject to much passionate debate in trans circles. We say it as a short-cut phrase, rarely bothering to go deeper and explain what we really mean with those words. Whenever I talk to cis people about what it's like to be trans, this is the main stumbling block I come to: the overwhelming, life-ruining phenomenon of dysphoria, and how hard it can be to recognise this force without having experienced it. People who have not, who are apt to disbelieve those who have, talk about it as something cosmetic and superficial. Sometimes, offering pity without understanding, they characterise it as a feeling akin to the self-loathing brought on by comparisons of the self to unrealistic, photoshopped images of models and movie stars.

I cannot talk about my experiences of dysphoria without first talking about proprioception. Proprioception broadly translates to the sense we have of the body as a physical entity: its position in space, a sensory map, its relationship to itself. It is what allows us to move without watching that movement, to truly inhabit our own physicality in a physical world. It's crucial to our spatial awareness.

What dysphoria has always felt like to me is a clash between what my body knows *should* be there – the sexed characteristics that I can feel through proprioception – and the sexed characteristics that, bizarrely, impossibly, seem actually to exist. It's like missing a step in the dark, when you're convinced that the step is actually there until the moment you hit the ground. It's not wanting a different body: it's knowing how your body should be, and living with the continual pain of discord, as wrong as a broken bone. I didn't make changes to my sexed body so as to conform to gendered ideas of what that body should look like. I did it so that I could finally be complete in myself, and free from the shock of being divided in presence that had plagued me since I entered puberty. My proprioceptive sex was and is just as real to me as any other part of me – more real, in fact, than aspects of my physicality I genuinely could not feel and could not find on my mental map. Coming into myself after physical transition was the most extraordinary sensation; my mother, seeing my face for the first time after surgery, said she had never seen me smile so wholeheartedly before. It was like waking up well after interminable illness. Not only my mental health improved: with a body that I finally felt free in I could breathe, sing, move in ways I just didn't know existed. This sense of grounding, of wholeness, has nothing to do with the insecurities I carry about my appearance – insecurities common to many and culturally shaped – and everything to do with finally feeling *right* in my own particular, imperfect and perfect way.

This sensation, of a proprioceptive sex at odds with the external body, is not common to all trans people. Trans is, after all, an incredibly broad term. But it is common, and seems, when discussed, remarkably similar in how it manifests. In her groundbreaking work *Whipping Girl*, biologist and activist Julia Serano refers to this sense as 'subconscious sex'. She writes:

> Perhaps the best way to describe how my subconscious sex feels to me is to say that it seems as if, on some level, my brain expects my body to be female. Indeed, there is some evidence to suggest that our brains have an intrinsic understanding of what sex our bodies should be ... When one's subconscious and conscious sexes match, as they do for cissexuals, an appropriate gender identity may emerge rather seamlessly. For me, the tension I felt between these two disparate understandings of myself was wholly jarring ...

Despite the recent popularity of 'mindfulness' and 'full body wellness', society still, frequently, insists on the division between the mind and the body. We dismiss conditions we do not like to admit of – depression, chronic pain, undiagnosed disabilities – with the phrase 'it's just in your head', as if the head were disconnected from the rest of us. We ignore all that we know of body–mind interaction, and of the physicality of brain states and mental processing both, because it is easier to refer to the under-researched and inexplicable as madness.

But we can't talk about the sexed body without talking about *all* of the body – the brain included. And, in turn, we cannot talk about the body without considering how it is we know that body to exist, how the mind tells us what we know. Sex is not just what is seen by an outside observer – it's how the body knows itself. And for trans people who have experienced dysphoria, we *know* that how we know ourselves is a unique phenomenon in need of acknowledgement.

Trans people have been providing evidence of their experience of dysphoria, of proprioceptive or subconscious sex, for more than a century.

If we would dismiss the chance to learn more, then we admit to caring less about scientific inquiry than we do about the gendered stereotypes of sex.

But even when we open our minds to the validity of trans-related information, we run into problems. It's not enough that we open up trans lives to scientific inquiry – not if, in so doing, we are merely repeating cultural clichés about gender, now dressed up by lab coats and tables of data.

A vital point, when considering sex, is one that has been made over and over again by scientists, by philosophers of science, by sociologists and historians of science: that we cannot divorce a singular, unified 'Science' from the broader cultures that create and sustain it. What we observe, what we think about what we observe, how we analyse our thoughts, what we pass on to others, are all shaped by cultural forces beyond our personal control.

There is the deeper, older, ongoing debate about how scientific investigation should proceed, and what it is we mean by those terms. The works of Karl Popper, the Science Wars of the late twentieth century, the challenges of Thomas Kuhn and Paul Feyerabend: a slight introduction to an enormous, ongoing learning process.

And there is also the specific point crucial to any understanding of the science of sex, obvious but so often unchallenged: that what we 'know' about sex – even when we think we know it empirically, logically – is so often just a reflection of what we want to know, or the confirmation of unexamined biases. Much of philosopher Judith Butler's works have been devoted to questioning and unpicking this inscription of meaning onto the world around us, but we do not have to be philosophers to recognise how often we are misled by our own prejudices – and use those prejudices, in turn, to mislead others.

When trying to examine this phenomenon, it can be easier to start with the past, for two reasons. Firstly, to shatter the assumption that our ideas now are based on some unchanging, eternal fact. But also, and almost more importantly, to allow the clarity of hindsight and distance to teach us how to see the ways in which the cultural beliefs of every era informed what that era knew about sex. And, in so doing, to acknowledge the ways in which we fall into the same trap.

Possibly the most surprising fact about sex in Western history is that even our most basic assumption – that there are two opposite sexes – is a relatively modern invention. Many scholars believe that, for much of our recent past, we did not so much follow a two-sex binary model as a one-sex hierarchical one. British historian Laura Gowing explains the Galenic mode, the prevailing sex theory before the eighteenth century, as having male and female as two opposite points on a scale, with hermaphrodites (an archaic term for intersex people) falling in the middle. American scholar Kathryn Ringrose elaborates on this explanation: that the one-sexed model can be seen as a kind of ladder. At the top, you have the virile, manly, 'perfect' man, and at the bottom, you have women. This perfect man is the ideal embodiment of the human animal and woman, as in Aristotle's theories, is the imperfect failure of type. But this model contains its own warning – this is a ladder, after all. One can climb up or fall down. So it is that gendered behaviour can change the sexed body and, therefore, that gendered behaviour must be policed.

We can find countless examples of how gendered behaviour was seen to have affected sex changes: in Greek culture, Roman history, the Byzantine Empire, in the bodies of Christian saints, medieval sinners and in the studies of Renaissance and Enlightenment men of letters. One of my favourites is recorded by one Dr Carr in his *Medical Epistles*. He writes of two nuns who, due to their excessive masturbation (manly behaviour), and probable masturbation of each other (even worse manly behaviour), caused their clitorises to grow into penises, were expelled from their convent, and ever afterwards presented themselves as men. As the clitoris and penis were held to be variations on the same theme – as we now know they are – it did not seem too far-fetched to claim that manipulating the clitoris in a supposedly masculine fashion could cause it to grow.

While the one-sex model slowly gave way to the new binary system, the belief that the body was still sexed along a continuum, and could be altered by gender variance (in practice or thought), was still with us well into the nineteenth and twentieth centuries. We can look back now and dismiss such theories, in the same way that we dismiss equally popular scientific beliefs in phrenology and eugenics – but can we afford to dismiss what we can learn from these failures?

The evidence that gender changed sex was, supposedly, easy to find, and easy to document through self-described rigorous, impartial methods. In 1802 George Cabanis, a physiologist, medical professor and philosopher, wrote that male inverts (a category of person neither gay nor trans in our parlance, but approximating a combination of the two) had the bone structure of 'normal' women, particularly in the pelvis. Perhaps the most extreme example of this form of reasoning can be found in the works of Ambroise Tardieu, a medical doctor and one of the most important forensic medical scientists of the nineteenth century. His 1857 forensic handbook, *Etude Médico-Légale sur les Attentats aux Mœurs*, was a bestseller, translated into all major European languages. He believed that he had proof that inverted gendered practices or underlying tendencies changed the sexed bodies of inverts in the most extreme of ways. Historian Graham Robb describes some of his claims here – 'pederast' was nineteenth-century French slang for a man who desired men.

Tardieu ... believed that passive pederasts had enormous bottoms: 'I have seen one pederast whose buttocks were joined and formed a single, perfect sphere.' In active pederasts, the penis was deformed: it bulged like a snout or tapered like a dog's penis and, for a reason easily imagined, it had a distinctive corkscrew shape as a result, pederasts were unable to urinate in a straight line.

I believe that physicians now would be hard-pressed to find the physical examples Tardieu claimed to have observed, and to have observed in such numbers so as to have formed a type. But Tardieu *did* claim to have seen them, to have studied them, and his findings were accepted and celebrated by his peers. I don't write this here in an attempt to mock researchers in the past – although I have to admit to finding some of it rather funny – but to make the point that every mind, no matter how brilliant, is subject to the culture that created it. We must never believe that we are unaffected by our own current folklore of gender, in the false confidence that we are better than our forebears.

After all, this kind of sexed myth-making has continued long into the twentieth century.

When I was growing up the existence of the hymen was a fact. The 'guide to your changing body' my parents bought me said that the hymen could be torn through sex or sport, or gradually worn away with time, but that it was definitely there – a thin membrane stretching across the vaginal opening. But, recently, many sex researchers believe that the hymen as we think of it – a seal that, once torn, cannot be repaired, named after the Greek god of marriage – does not exist. Rather, there is the vaginal corona: a remnant of fetal development only present in some people, made up of elastic mucous membrane just inside the vaginal opening.

The bodily importance of the vaginal corona seems minimal – but the cultural importance of the hymen, its utility as a tool with which to enact gendered laws, is still with us. 'Virginity tests', in which fingers or another implement are inserted into a woman's vagina to see if she has a hymen, are still carried out in all parts of the world. Amnesty

International has described these tests as a form of torture. 'Virginity tests' are used as a way of keeping women in their place, of punishing those who step out of line and of enforcing social order. This is not some medieval fantasy of bloody sheets displayed after the consummation of a royal marriage, or something that Westerners can claim only happens 'over there'. British immigration officers were ordering doctors to carry out virginity tests on migrant women as recently as 1979. Young people are still being taught that there is a part of their bodies that can 'prove' their sexual status as virgins, another tricky concept. Sexed bodies are no match for gendered expectations, when those expectations uphold what is considered right, and normal.

And those gendered expectations are still affecting scientific research, and our ideas of the 'truth' of sex, in the here and now.

Research from Newcastle University, published in 2007 in *Current Biology*, claimed that women had a deep-seated preference for pink and that 'this preference has an evolutionary advantage behind it'. The researchers behind this study suggested that this preference for pink could have come from a hunter-gatherer division of labour in our distant past. If men hunted and women gathered, then women could have developed a preference for pink so as to find the ripest berries. This conclusion, and the research that they believed backed it up, was widely feted by the press. 'Women may be hardwired to prefer pink' according to *New Scientist* and, from *The Times*, 'At last, science discovers why blue is for boys but girls really do prefer pink'.

The study assumes much about unknown aspects of early human society and behaviour; it is extraordinary that this research, and the reporting of it, didn't examine what the historical record shows: that pink has only been associated with girls in the past hundred years. American Studies professor Jo B. Paoletti has charted the history of the gendering of the colours pink and blue, finding that, prior to the solidifying of 'blue for boys, pink for girls' in the 1940s, things were often more mixed up, or even the other way around. Science writer Ben Goldacre, in his critique of this study, included advice from the *Sunday Sentinel* in 1914 and the *Ladies' Home Journal* in 1918, in which mothers were told to dress their little boys in pink (a stronger colour) and their girls in blue (daintier and more delicate).

The interpretation of this study's findings was so in keeping with what we want to believe about the gendered nature of sex, and the sexed basis of gender, that critical analysis and a true examination of *all* data were forgotten. This study is one of many – and each new study treated in this way goes on to further strengthen those cultural stereotypes, that in turn produce more suspect research and unexamined interpretations.

We must be aware of all of these factors if we are to try to examine trans people's experiences of sex in a scientific way. And, crucially, we must own and acknowledge these factors when we see 'Science' used to dismiss and erase trans experiences altogether.

All ages believe themselves to be modern. All ages look back on the same claim made by ages past and laugh at the supposed arrogance in the comparison, forgetting how we will appear to the future.

My final point is a simple one: that when it comes to what

we know about sex, what we need most is humility. We do not know it all yet. We do not even know how little we know. We demand surety, when all that we have is open-ended investigation, still in its infancy. It's terrifying and thrilling, and too vast to be summed up by closed conclusions and closed minds.

The sad fact is that, more often than not, those who most want to claim that we know all there is to know about sex aren't even aware of how little it is that we know, and how much that little has changed. In popular culture – in the media, in schools, in the workplace, even in hospitals and doctors' surgeries – we talk about 'facts' which 'everybody knows', without examining what it is we've actually learnt in an examined way compared to what we've picked up through ingrained assumptions and cultural conditioning. We often talk about 'biological sex' using the examples we were taught in high school, and actively refuse the need to learn more and learn better.

When it comes to the impact of sex on trans lives, and what trans lives can tell us of what sex is, we have to stop pretending that we know all there is to know and focus instead on learning more.

Sex is a shifting, evolving, ever-expanding term that needs to reflect the totality of our bodies and bodily experiences, and to do so in a way that allows for human error and shortsightedness.

It is not a trump card to deny the existence of trans lives.

6

Think of the Children

Even people who support trans adults and our medical needs can balk at the idea of the existence of trans children, let alone the fact that they may need medical care. I understand that. If what I knew about the subject came from general reporting, and not personal knowledge, I might be worried, too. There are the attention-grabbing headlines, of course: the ones about 'sex changes' for toddlers, and 'transgender hormones' for pre-teens. There's the incredible increase in the number of young people and their families seeking referrals to gender identity clinics, and dubious theories as to why that might be. Everyone can remember at least one time when they were young and headstrong and thought they would want something new for ever, only to get bored with it in a week or two. Opponents of trans people capitalise on those memories. It is right that we should be worried about young people, but there is also a danger that those worries could actually be making life harder for the very children in question.

First, some facts: what do we mean when we say trans children, and what do we mean when we talk about treatment?

Crucially, when talking about young people, the term 'gender non-conforming' is used, rather than trans. The reasons are twofold: to try to describe without pathologising or locking into a specific category, and because the children being referred to gender specialists, who are being described, express a broad range of behaviours and reported beliefs about their own selves. A gender non-conforming child could be a child challenging traditional ideas of gender expression: a little boy who is adamant that he wants to wear dresses and be a princess. A gender non-conforming child could also be a child insisting that their gender is different from the one they were assigned at birth: a child who insists that he is a boy, despite being told by everyone else that he's actually a girl. Or, of course, a gender non-conforming child could be a mixture of these things: a child who knows that they are neither a boy nor a girl, who refuses the sex they were assigned at birth and a host of gendered expectations. Some children and adolescents are clear in naming themselves trans. Others are not: they agree that they are the sex they were assigned at birth, but not to the gendered expectations of what that sex should mean. The main reason this category is so large is because of the various motivations parents have for bringing their children to medical attention. Some parents are concerned that their children are not developing along normative gendered lines, and want that child to be encouraged to change their behaviour to better fit societal mores. Other parents seek out a gender specialist because that child is in pain from their bodily dysphoria, and from being classed as the wrong gender. I note these differences here, because they make a big difference to later arguments over some of the most controversial research in the area.

When we talk about treatment what we're mostly talking about is the emotional and practical guidance families need to help them to support their children, and the counselling and group therapy that may be required to help a child who feels depressed, isolated and in need of reassurance and care. There are additional options for teenagers and young adults, but emotional support is at the heart of caring for gender non-conforming youth.

A representative of the TransYouth project at the University of Washington explains:

> Our experience is that everyone gets nervous when 5-year-olds are mentioned in the same sentence or paragraph as hormones and surgery — and for good reason. Once again, though, care is needed in interpretation. First, and most critically, the only intervention that is being made with prepubescent transgender children is a social, reversible, non-medical one — allowing a child to change pronouns, hairstyles, clothes, and a first name in everyday life. No one in mainstream medicine (or elsewhere, to our knowledge) is performing surgery on or providing hormones to prepubescent transgender children.

There's a line I've heard from multiple trans people about the double bind of age and the acceptable trans narrative: to get access to treatment as an adult, you have to have known you were trans since early childhood. But if you say that you're trans in early childhood, you're told that you're too young to know.

When we ask trans adults when they first knew that they

were trans, the majority will say that they knew as children. They may not have had the words, but they recognised that there was something about them that made them markedly different. Natacha Kennedy of Goldsmith's University, London, is one of the leading researchers into the experience of gender non-conforming youth, particularly in educational contexts, and into the childhood experiences of trans adults. Her 2012 study, 'Transgender children: more than a theoretical challenge', cuts deep for me; reading the experiences gathered there was an exercise in old pain. Kennedy found that, while a majority of trans adults become aware of their transness at a young age, an average of eight years old, they were also aware that that knowledge was shameful and needed to be hidden away from their friends and families. Not knowing how to understand their own feelings, many first believed that God had made a mistake, before coming to understand that they must be the ones who are wrong, mistaken. The average time span between realisation and verbalisation – learning any words other than insults and abuse with which to name the trans experience – was seven and a half years. Before they found that language, the huge majority of respondents felt like they were the only ones in the whole world to feel as they did.

My childhood was atypical in a number of aspects, and I know that the ways in which my parents did gender was one of the main ones. I am so very grateful for that. It's a standard question to ask: 'When did you know?' People ask it of me, and they ask it of my parents. And I think I like my mother's answer the best: 'We were learning as we went along.' But, for far too long, I still felt the shame of being different: a failure, a freak, and alone.

At home I was never made to feel as though there was something wrong about my behaviour, or that there was any gendered difference between the expectations placed upon my brother and myself: that we would be kind, and honest, and try our best. So I was allowed to dress up in my father's clothes, and dress up in my mother's, and my brother and I pooled a collection of variously gendered toys with which to create elaborate set pieces and storylines. I very much liked shiny, glittery things and pretty dresses, and also being the biggest, strongest kid in the playground who could beat everyone at arm wrestling. When my father went away on business my brother and I would practise shaving our faces with his razors, foam and cologne. When my father was feeling particularly generous, we would practise face painting on him. I never had the impression that there were things boys should do and things girls should do at home, and when I heard that kind of attitude at school I was outraged. Joan of Arc was my hero, and I had an active fantasy life in which I was transformed into a stern and androgynous warrior with elaborate armour, and a white steed.

It was puberty that let me know that I was trans. First the dysphoria and then, crucially, the lack of any knowledge of people like me, and the societal approbation for all the ways in which I wasn't 'normal'. Between the onset of puberty, at the age of eight, and the point at which I had the beginnings of language about myself, at fifteen, I veered between denial, self-hatred and terror. It's a tribute to my family that, alongside all of those negatives, I also knew that I was loved, and still believed in their belief in me. It's a typical and an atypical trans narrative, and it's for those reasons that I share it. Because many of us did and do know young, and many of us suffer alone, unable to reach out. But also because what we can receive from those around us – unconditional love, unwavering belief – can carry us through to a better future.

By listening to, and believing, the young people who say that they are trans, we have the chance to end that pattern of isolation and self-loathing, to make the experience of being unconditionally loved the norm, rather than the exception. Removing stigma and sharing knowledge is not the same as forcing a label or category onto a young person. And if there are gender clinics willing to help families, and society, towards a place of openness, wisdom and care then we should all be grateful.

As to why there are more openly trans young people now than there ever were before, the answer would seem to be obvious. There is constant talk about how society has shifted in terms of trans acceptance, knowledge about trans issues, visibility of trans people. This media moment is a symptom of something much deeper, and more profound: the year on year work undertaken by activists working in the fields of health care, legal change, community support, education and outreach. Slowly, we are (at least in some fields) gaining wider support, a more legitimate voice in a broader culture. In her work, Natacha Kennedy describes the importance of 'key words': words and phrases which allow a young person to recognise themselves and find others like them, unlocking knowledge of trans existence. Is it any wonder that, in a world where trans people are more widely seen and believed, children who may be trans will have earlier access to the words that help them describe themselves?

These cultural shifts do not impact on trans people alone. After all, trans children do not appear out of thin air. A change in parental attitudes would cause a significant change in the recording of numbers of trans youth. Trans people have, historically, been highly likely to experience family rejection and physical and emotional abuse from parents. Homelessness is a serious problem for trans teenagers, and stories of violence are common. What if this shift in numbers is simply this generation of parents doing better by their trans children?

As ever, though, this change can't happen fast enough. While conversion therapy is fading out of practice in the treatment of trans adults, it's all too often the first port of call for families looking to have their child 'fixed' of their transgressive behaviour.

The death of American teenager Leelah Alcorn at the very end of 2014 sent shock waves across social media, following the publication of her suicide note on Tumblr. A trans girl with unsupportive parents, Leelah had been forced into conversion therapy to try to change a fundamental aspect of who she was. Her initial plans to wait it out and transition when she was free of her parents' control couldn't withstand the constant pressure to be other than she was. Before taking her own life she wrote: 'My death needs to mean something. My death needs to be counted in the number of transgender people who commit suicide this year. Fix society. Please.'

Leelah Alcorn is one of many. Every trans person I know will have their own stories of suicides in our communities. Many of us will have personal stories to tell of times when death seemed like the only option. Living in a transphobic world is hard on any adult. For an adolescent with no wider support network, subject to constant cruelty at school and at home, the pain can often be unbearable. Conversion therapy can be, is, the final straw.

There are parents like Leelah Alcorn's, who cannot stand to see their child live a truth that runs contrary to their religious or cultural beliefs. They choose conversion therapy in the hope of salvation. Other parents will be driven by a desire to avoid the shame of having a trans child, or by ideological views about gender just as strong as religious fervour.

There are many parents who do not care whether a child is trans or not, but who push for conversion therapy because any behaviour which challenges gender norms is an embarrassment, or a threat, to be 'fixed'.

And then there are interested observers, outsiders, who, lacking personal experience, support conversion therapy because they believe the widely touted claim that the majority of gender non-conforming youth will never transition, will change their minds of their own accord and turn out to be, more or less, 'normal'.

In this framing, adult trans people are claiming that these young people are also trans to further a political cause or promote an ideology, with no respect for what it is that these kids actually need. Several UK journalists have described treatment for trans children as child abuse. It reminds me of nothing so much as the scaremongering over the myth that gay men, bisexual people and lesbians recruit children to the 'gay lifestyle' because we are sinister, predatory and, supposedly, can't have kids of our own.

If that were actually the case, it would be an outrage – but it's simply not true. It's an enticing message, playing as it does on pre-existing prejudices, but try to find some supporting evidence and you'll come up cold. American advocate Brynn Tannehill explains:

The most cited study (Steensma) which alleges an 84 percent desistance rate, did not actually differentiate between children with consistent, persistent and insistent gender dysphoria, kids who socially transitioned, and kids who just acted more masculine or feminine than their birth sex and culture allowed for. In other words, it treated gender non-conformance the same as gender dysphoria. Worse, the study could not locate 45.3 percent of the children for follow up, and made the assumption that all of them were desisters. Indeed, other studies used to support this also suffered from similar methodological flaws. As a result, the 84 percent desistance figure is meaningless, since both the numerator and denominator are unknown, because you have no idea how many of the kids ended up transitioning (numerator), and no idea how many of them were actually gender dysphoric to begin with (denominator). When Dr. Steensma went back in 2013 and looked at the intensity of dysphoria these children felt as a factor in persistence, it turned out that it was actually a very good predictor of which children would transition. In other words, the children who actually met the clinical guidelines for gender dysphoria as children generally ended up as transgender adults. Further research has shown that children who meet the clinical guidelines for gender dysphoria are as consistent in their gender identity as the general population.

I consider reparative treatments – which, being based on trying to change a child's gendered behaviour, in my view seek to shame them into conformity, and to restructure love and support as something conditionally granted in exchange for compliance and denial of self – are not just harmful for trans youth, not just harmful for all gender non-conforming children and teenagers, but a gross betrayal of the Hippocratic injunction to do no harm. That's not a medical treatment – that's brainwashing and emotional abuse.

The alternative to this is what is known as gender affirming therapy. Texas-based clinical psychologist Dr Colt Keo-Meier explains:

> The gender affirmative model supports identity exploration and development without an a priori goal of any particular gender identity or expression. Practitioners of the gender affirmative model do not push children in any direction, rather, they listen to children and, with the help of parents, translate what the child is communicating about their gender identity and expression. They work toward improving gender health, where a child is able to live in the gender that feels most authentic to the child and can express gender without fear of rejection.

We can support children without pathologising them, and can allow them to express themselves without external pressure to fit into one category or another. We could show parents how to provide that support, and allowance for exploration, at home. We can organise youth groups and support circles, where children and parents can meet others in similar situations, can reach out and not feel quite so alone.

And for those who need them – and remember that not all trans people need hormones or surgery – we can make sure that age-appropriate hormonal and surgical options are available. This is the particular point that causes so much outrage, so much anger. As ever, the reality is far less frightening than the headline spin. The hormone treatments known as puberty blockers have been in use for a long time, long before they were prescribed to some trans teenagers. The whole point of puberty blockers is that they are reversible; they were developed to treat children who enter puberty at a very young age, to allow them the time to wait and grow and start developing at the same age as their peers at eleven or twelve years old, as opposed to four or five. For trans children who have expressed a deep and persistent need to physically transition, puberty blockers are a godsend: a chance to take the time to explore their options, to settle on what they need, and an opportunity to avoid the psychological and physical agony of experiencing the wrong puberty. When these teenagers are older, around the age of sixteen – the same age at which they could join the army, get married or create a child – then they can, with close supervision, begin hormone therapy. When they reach the age eighteen they can, as any other adult, choose to pursue surgery. I cannot see what is controversial about this. It is a careful, conservative approach to supporting those, and only those, who actively seek out medical transition. And, from the research we have, it seems to be working incredibly well.

The most important research to date (there is now a fair amount, all positive) appeared in 2014, a longitudinal study of fifty-five young adults in the Netherlands who had been diagnosed with gender dysphoria and treated under the gender affirmative model, with the use of puberty blockers beginning around the age of fourteen. Participants went on to pursue surgery, at an average age of twenty-one. At the time of the study, these young people 'were no longer experiencing mental health consequences related to gender dysphoria, their quality of life and happiness levels were on par with their non-transgender peers, and none expressed any regret about delaying puberty or transitioning'. A 2015 study from the Rady's Children Hospital in San Diego found much the same thing. Of the forty-two young people who had sought treatment, including puberty blockers for young teenagers and hormone therapy for older teenagers, none had expressed regret or wanted to stop treatment. Significant improvements to mental health were found across the board.

The research is ongoing; the US National Institute for Health commenced the largest ever study of trans youth at the beginning of 2016, which will take at least another six years to complete. We don't have all the answers yet; as with any evolving aspect of human nature, it is unlikely that we will ever hold all the answers. But we know enough now to understand how harmful conversion therapy is, how pointless, compared with the alternatives on offer. If the wellbeing of our young people is truly our greatest concern, we should follow the research, and not our own fears and prejudices.

Still, despite the data, there will be those who believe that this is all too risky, that it's unacceptable to allow children to pursue any path that they might later come to regret, even if the actual risk of regret seems negligible. From my perspective, this seems to display a deliberate blindness to the wide number of risks we already allow children to take, that we encourage them to take.

There was a moment of risk-taking in my own childhood that I would not have taken if I had known what would follow. But because it was considered a normal level and category of risk there were no warnings, and nobody tried to dissuade my parents from allowing me what I wanted.

I broke my right wrist at the age of eleven, falling off a horse. It was a very bad break, and I was already firmly committed to pursuing a career as a professional pianist; it had been an overwhelming ambition throughout my childhood, and my teachers were both confident in and encouraging of this ambition. I had started riding because that's what the popular kids did at my school, and I wanted to fit in, to make the children who hated me accept me as one of their own. The children's ward I ended up in, preparing for and recovering from emergency surgery, had several other patients who had been injured by horses: one young girl, the same age as me, had had her pelvis crushed after the pony she was riding had reared up and fallen on her – she would never be able to bear children. The doctor who treated me told my parents that horse riding was more risky than riding a motorbike, and that he would ban it if he could.

I needed two further operations on my wrist, a handful of invasive procedures under local anesthetic, and years of intensive rehabilitation. Throughout those years, I kept training, kept playing, up until the point where I could no longer move my fingers. I was accepted onto one of the most prestigious music courses at a British university – I spent the first two years in a haze of pain medication, depression and despair. Eventually, after a great deal of uncertainty, time off for treatments, and more time off to recover from those treatments, I regained the limited use of my right hand. It wasn't enough. Popular wisdom at the time held that trans people on hormone replacement therapy would in all likelihood lose their singing voices completely; my voice was the only instrument left to me. I retrained as a classical singer, at the cost of treating my dysphoria completely. I learnt to work around my chronic pain to the point of being able to play simple piano accompaniments, and to work around my dysphoria with non-hormonal treatments and a wonderful support network. Losing both of those dreams at once was, and is, a constant struggle.

Maybe you think that these two examples – of musical vocation, and transition – are incompatible. I do not think that they are. My sense of myself as a musician – the constant internal music playing, the need to express it, the joy of sitting down at the keys and playing without thinking, without being anything but the physical embodiment of something far greater and more beautiful than I could ever hope to be – this is who I am at the core. It is so much more important to my sense of self than my sense of gender, my sexed body, and those things are pretty foundational.

The hypocrisy in telling young people who are genuinely desperate for treatment that it's too risky for them to have it – even after they have jumped through so many safeguarding hoops – while sanctioning, encouraging, other kinds of risk distresses me. It has everything to do with cultural norms, and nothing to do with keeping children safe while still allowing them their autonomy. We have to move forward from the idea that it is somehow a shame, a failure, for a child to grow up to be trans. We have to start approaching this subject with young people's best interests at heart, not our own concerns and judgements about how we would want our children to conform. Being trans is not a fate anyone needs saving from. But everyone, every child, needs to be loved for who they truly are, without conditions.

7

Delusional and Disturbed

The accusation, the insinuation, that being trans is a form of madness is one with an answer that comes at a personal cost. To answer it fully requires an admission, a detailing of my history of mental illness, and a tallying of the ways in which it and my transness can appear to cross over, but are not the same. Both of those traits are stereotyped and demonised away from their lived realities. In giving that answer, I know that it can be so easily used as a false affirmative: yes, they are mad, because they admitted they're mad, and that means that the delusion of being trans is a form of madness, because mad people believe it. I've used kinder language and the correct pronouns, but you get the idea. Honesty in one area is used to discredit it in another. Being trans is often believed to cause mental illness, and mental illness to cause the belief of being trans.

The cost of this belief is twofold. It becomes a way of dismissing trans people, of labelling us 'insane', and denying our right to live honest lives. But it also prevents trans people from seeking, and acquiring, help for genuine mental health problems, out of fear that our transness will be blamed, our medical and social care withheld.

It is because of that myth, and that double stigma, that I want to be honest about my own experiences.

I had a breakdown when I was thirteen years old, and have been in and out of treatment, mostly in, ever since. After an initial, disastrous experience with a private psychoanalyst, recommended by the doctor who had dismissed my distress, I spent four years under the care of Child and Adolescent Mental Health Services at St George's Hospital in London. I genuinely cannot imagine being here without their help. Twice a week at the beginning, and then once a week, once a fortnight when I was doing better, my mother would pick me up from school and we would drive to the hospital for appointments with my psychological team, psychiatrist and cognitive behavioural therapist. When one treatment failed, they tried another. When I couldn't continue without drugs, they prescribed them, and when those drugs became too much they helped me come off them. Before I started treatment I was sleeping two, maybe three hours a night, if I was lucky, and would spend around four hours each evening locked in the bathroom, washing and rewashing my hands, my body, the floor – everything. I was in constant physical pain from depression, and the waking nightmares that are the obsessional element of OCD made me believe that I was both evil to the point of being unsaveable, and dangerously close to losing all control over my own mind. After all, I had no control over the washing, checking and counting compulsions that left my skin bleeding and my bedroom full of odd stacks of items, placed in rows and only in certain numerical combinations. I wanted to live, but I didn't want the life I was living. The doctors who treated me gave me first the hope of something better, and then the tools with which to bring it into being.

I never told them I was trans, not even after I had come out at school and founded a national LGBT youth organisation. They never asked. I told myself at the time that it was because I didn't see my gender as an illness, something to be treated; I didn't need their help with being trans, so why would I bring it up? There's an element of truth in that. But what is also true is that I had no belief in their ability to acknowledge my gender while continuing my treatment, and feared that if I told them the truth they would take my treatment away. It was in the wording of the intake paperwork, an enormous form you fill in to give the team an idea of what they're meant to be treating. There was page after page of statements – 'I usually find it hard to make friends', 'I have less energy than I used to', those kinds of things – and you have to mark your response to each, from 'all the time' to 'not at all'. I forget the exact wording, but I remember the placement. Around halfway through the form, after 'I like to set fires' was written 'I want to be the opposite sex', or words to that effect. I remember hovering over that item, trying to marshal all of the vague questions, impulses, fantasies I'd experience up until that point into a suitable answer, but couldn't. I didn't know what would happen to me if I ticked 'all the time', 'most of the time', 'sometimes'. I didn't know how to express that I didn't want to be 'the opposite sex', but that it was likely that I was something else entirely, someone who wasn't a girl or a boy, and who thought the whole system needed changing. I imagined that, if I replied in

the affirmative, they might not be able to help me with the
nightmares, the pain in my chest, the way that my own mind
and body had turned against me. Without their help, I feared
I wouldn't have the strength to keep living. It felt safest all
round to tick 'not at all', and tell myself that I could figure it
out in my own time.

Maybe I misjudged my mental health team. I hope I did.
I certainly presented myself in all kinds of gender variant
ways, and their compassion and care never wavered. But,
even so, I listen to the horror stories of trans friends and
acquaintances. I have listened to tales of doctors who insist
on forcibly changing patients' gendered behaviour and presentation before providing help for PTSD, eating disorders
and schizophrenia; of doctors who have denied medication and counselling because they disapprove of their trans
patients. All of this, happening right now in 2016. Maybe as
a teenager in 1998 it was safest to err on the side of caution
and stay silent. But what a terrible choice to force a desperate
person to make.

It is not only that mental health care can be cut off for being
trans, but that transition-related care can be cut off for being
mentally ill. Any sign that we are less than 100 per cent mentally well and adjusted – as though such a person exists – and
access to hormones, to surgery, can be instantly denied.
There is such a strong belief that believing oneself to be any
gender other than that you were assigned at birth is itself a
sign of psychosis, that trans people have to prove themselves
to be saner than sane in order to be believed.

The roots of the myth of trans insanity go back a long
way. Parmenides and Herodotus described 'the Scythians'

madness' as a congenital, inheritable mental disease that caused men to speak, dress and act like women. Cross-gendered behaviour was seen as a sin, but also as a form of madness, throughout much of Western history. The originators of the modern disciplines of psychology and psychiatry as we know them today were fascinated by the idea of criminal types, moral insanity and the hopeless degeneracy of the mind that would lead to anti-social behaviours, including those behaviours we would now describe as trans. In the popular imagination any hint of queerness – inappropriately gendered behaviour – could function as a code for dangerous madness. Pulp fiction and schlock horror have had their share of proto-trans villains; cross-gendered behaviour could function as a signal for martyrdom or villainy. *The Rocky Horror Show*'s murderous Doctor Frank-N-Furter was a deliberate parody of these pop culture monsters. Trans characters make for good serial killers in the minds of cis creators, presented as men who want to wear the clothes or skins of women: *Psycho*, *Dressed to Kill*, *The Silence of the Lambs*. The discredited theory of autogynephilia, the idea that trans women are really men who get a sexual kick out of trying to inhabit the bodies of women, has a cultural debt to pay to these depictions.

Conversion therapy could not exist without the belief that being trans is a delusion, a sickness to be cured. It was the rationale behind the electro-shock treatments, the enforced isolation, the committing to mental institutions. Trans legend April Ashley was, in her youth, hospitalised and injected with sodium pentothal and testosterone. Up until the 1980s, some clinicians still recommended the use of nausea-inducing drugs in the 'aversion' treatment of trans patients.

Strangers online like to tell me that I'm deluded. I realise that this is a fairly common experience now for anyone who seeks to pursue any kind of public career. But I do find it interesting that these strangers are so invested in diagnosing my state of mind from behind their keyboards, and wonder at the disgust with which they make such pronouncements. Another popular comment is that I've 'lost the plot', that too much time at university has muddled my brain, as though I were some overly ambitious Edwardian bluestocking, refusing to acknowledge her feminine limits. Opponents of trans people use many a dog-whistle term to indicate that we are not in our right minds: hysterical, unstable, extreme, fanatical.

I know of many trans people who have not been able to get referrals to specialist gender clinics because their GPs still believe that being trans is a form of make-believe, a fantasy invented by disturbed and dangerous people. I know some trans people who, while institutionalised, were forced to detransition, or hide their gender variance, before they were considered well enough to be released.

Maybe, in the interests of honesty, of unencumbered communication, I should try to answer that question from the inside. Is my belief that I am transgender and genderqueer – not a man and not a woman, but someone ill-suited to either descriptor, who deserves the right to shape their own sexed body – a symptom of an unwell mind?

There have been times in my life where I have felt on the edges of sanity: where I have lost control, lost perspective, been unable to do anything but travel through until I hit the other side. I believe that this aspect of my self is fundamentally different from my awareness of my gendered self, and my challenge to a gendered world. Not because my manic depression or my obsessive compulsive disorder are not part of me, though they did not feel as though they were part of me for a great many years, but because the knowledge of how my mind knows my body to be is so ... I don't even know how to put it. How do you describe the mind and body describing the mind and body? Maybe by saying that that part is as unremarkable and basic as my brown hair and freckles. It just *is*.

Being trans and being mentally ill have both been hard, in their own ways. Dysphoria *hurts*. Smashing up against the gendered limits of our society and being smacked back hurts more. There is no doubt that dealing with transphobia and dysphoria have added to my emotional burdens. But they are not the same as the aching pain and concurrent nothingness of a low, finding oneself unable to get off the floor from an impossible mixture of emptiness and agony. Being trans is not the same as being caught in the middle of a bad OCD attack, with a mind full of horrifying images, imprinted onto the visual presence of the actual world, caught in an unstoppable bodily rhythm of impulse, release, drive, impulse, release, drive. I remember weeping, washing my hands and arms for hours, totally unable to stop – rocking backwards and forwards in horror as my body moved of its own volition – a machine without a pilot. I also remember weeping over the claustrophobia, the unfairness, of a body that didn't match what I knew it should be. Those tears did not come from the same place. Being called a freak when I'm having a hard day, being told to kill myself, not getting a job I knew I was qualified for, being spat at in the street; when the hatred of others hits me I've sobbed at how hard it is to be trans. When those things happen, they make my mental health worse. But I don't think that this response is pathological, but normal, and to be expected.

I don't want to have to cut out such an important part of my experience in order to prove that my gender and body are valid, healthy and right. As with so much in my life, I need the ability to say 'I am all of these thing together – they do not cancel each other out, but they are not the same.'

I am not delusional for knowing myself, in all of my ill health, my uniqueness, perseverance and hard-won clarity.

8

A Different Approach

The factor that has the biggest positive impact on the mental health and wellbeing of trans people is the genuine support of friends and family. As with much of the official data on trans populations we currently possess, the majority of research is North American-based, but what that research shows ties strongly with community knowledge from across the world.

A 2012 report prepared for Children's Aid Society of Toronto found that trans kids with supportive parents had an attempted suicide rate of 4 per cent, compared with a 57 per cent rate for trans children without that support. Another new study, this time from the University of Washington, has found that trans kids with supportive parents have the same mental health outcomes as any other group of young people. For trans adults, it is not only having the support of others, but being able to support others in turn. Having a sense of purpose within a broader trans community and the two-way street of mutual care, is one of the most powerful ways of

combating the depression and anxiety that so often follows
on from prejudice and discrimination.

What I have learnt from research, I had already experienced first-hand.

My family moved around a lot when I was a child, and
I believe that that is one of the reasons why my brother,
Jonathan, and I were so close. When we had nobody else we
always had each other; besides that, he was so easy to like.
Our tastes ran close, and it was always more fun to be a team
than to be apart. We had other friends – good friends – but
none of them could match the ways that he and I could see
inside each other's heads and know exactly what to say to
make the other laugh or reach out to help when something
was wrong.

As far as experiences of bullying goes, I've been lucky,
compared to many trans people. I was never physically
attacked, never sexually abused, and, later, I did make
friends. It was hard, but it could have been much harder.

It began when I moved schools, again, at the age of nine,
and found myself marked as an outsider in more ways than
one. The way I talked – my voice too deep and my accent
unplaceable – and the way I looked, being so much taller and
more developed than the other children. It's a familiar story:
notes that called me a freak, a chorus of mooing whenever I
walked past the popular girls in the playground, comments
about my body, specifically how it was too large, and my face,
which was too ugly, and all the usual insults of bitch, pig and
the like. There were the ongoing, relentless, personal attacks,
and the impersonal cruelty from kids hoping to avoid the
bullies' attention. There were a few nights where I believed
that I didn't deserve to live, made phone calls to ChildLine,

had attacks of panic and hysteria. But at least I always had my sanctuary of my home, my family, my brother: a place to be safe.

My parents certainly hoped that things would get better as I got older, and they did – to some degree. I found friends, I found teachers I liked and, with the school collection of music practice rooms, I could lock myself away every lunch-time, hide from the other pupils and escape into the piano. The bullying from the other students ebbed and flowed. Sometimes it was overt, with my name and the words 'weirdo' or 'freak' scrawled on blackboards in enormous letters, loud public imitations of my voice, my mannerisms, upfront quest-ions about why I was queer, why I had to be so masculine. Most of the time it was just that low-grade level of disapproval and mockery many teenagers would recognise: the sudden silence when you enter a room, the public lack of invitation to a party that everyone else is invited to, quiet laughter when you raise your voice in class. I learnt how to hate as a reflexive, protective gesture and how to turn my self-loathing into a spur to ambition, two common responses.

The hardest part, though, the part that will be so famil-iar to other trans people, was the fact that it wasn't just my peers who rejected and judged me – it was some adults also. It can be easy, as adults ourselves, to forget or diminish the impact our stated beliefs and actions can have on teenag-ers. But those feelings of being disbelieved, disregarded and – sometimes – hated by those in positions of authority wore me down. I started doing more public activism: writ-ing for an international LGBT website, campaigning against Section 28, meeting with the London Assembly. At every point where I tried to stand up for myself, it felt like there was someone older ready to smack me back down. I wanted so badly to be immune to what was said to me and said about me, but between the mixed states, the lows, the panic attacks, OCD attacks and constant, nagging dysphoria, I just didn't have the strength

Jonathan was my anchor when it would have been so easy to be washed away. It was a struggle to wake up every morning, to learn how to deal with conditions my doctors had told me would be lifelong, to learn how to bear the ridicule and disgust that seemed the inevitable reactions to being myself. I had ambitions, I had things that I loved but, against that constant pain, it was often hard to hold onto something as nebulous as a hope that it would get better, or a daydream about my future career. Sometimes, I couldn't imagine how things could be different, and sometimes I felt as though I didn't deserve to live.

Instead of the possibility of a better life *one day*, my brother gave me a better life *now*. He was the noisy, insistent reminder that I was not without ties to the world around me, that I was more than just an unwilling passenger in a life I didn't choose. He made me laugh despite myself, joke despite myself, gave me a space to unload my anger, gave me a chance to be frivolous and playful when everything else was grey and cold. He knew when to ask, and when to listen, and sensed when I couldn't talk but needed to be heard, silently.

More than that, he made demands on me. Not rudely or obviously, but in constant little ways. Could I, who found English easy, help him, who was dyslexic, with his homework? Could we write a screenplay together, to see if we could, and then make our millions? Could we go out for coffee, could I make that cake that he liked so much for his birthday, could he borrow a CD of a band we listened to together on MTV? Some of my happiest memories are of the evenings we spent, him lying in bed, me on the floor by the door, reading him the latest book in our favourite series, doing all of the voices. We were much too old for bedtime stories, but it became one of our rituals. It is a very powerful thing, when you feel at your lowest point, to know that someone else depends upon you. Not in a way that burdens you with expectations, or makes you feel ashamed for not being perfect, but in a way that says 'your life makes my life better – thank you for being here'. No matter how terrible, how disposable I felt, he gave me constant reassurance that who I was had value. In that mutual exchange of care, I felt the proof that his world, at least, was better for the fact that I was fighting to stay alive.

I suspect it was our relationship that primed me for wanting to do something to help other people, to do something, no matter how small, to be useful. I don't claim to be any kind of saint – I fuck up, and will keep fucking up, despite my best efforts and a great deal of guilt – but I believe I have done some little good along the way as well.

It has certainly taken me full circle in a way I never expected it would, and given me an idea for something else that might make things a little better for trans people like me.

When I got an email from my old school last year, I felt as though I'd stepped into a fictionalised version of my own life. In careful, respectful words, it asked me if I might have the time to prepare and give an assembly to the students

and teachers about how best to support trans students, and
to combat bullying and prejudice in general. The student
body was setting up an LGBT association, and the teachers
wanted to bring in an outside speaker as a show of support.
They had no idea I had been a pupil; they had found my contact details through my work in educational outreach. Nearly
all of the old staff were long gone. When I explained how bad
it had been for me they sympathised and apologised, and said
they were trying to make things better for the next generation of pupils. There was clearly a new approach in play.

I had my first panic attack in several years on my way
back to school. Walking through the gates, up to the main
hall, was an exercise in confusion; I'd had regular nightmares
about being trapped in my old school at least once a week for
the twelve years since I left. In those dreams, every detail
was perfect, every physical sensation hyper-real. Actually
being there left me feeling as exposed, as vulnerable, as if
I'd just woken up from one of those dreams. By the time I
was ready to get on stage I had sweated through the shirt I'd
worn, was very grateful for the blazer above it, and felt far
more nervous than I would before performing a show. I gave
my speech; to my astonishment, the teenagers in front of me
actually knew a great deal about trans people already. They
were friendly, attentive and had some wonderful things to
say of their own. Further adding to my sense of unreality, the
head teacher apologised for the bad time I'd had as a student,
and gave a short speech about how much they wanted to support their current pupils. Most importantly, for me, was what
happened as I was leaving. One of the younger students,
ducking out of a group on their way back to class, came over
to thank me; one of her friends, she explained, was trans, and

it was brilliant that people were talking more openly about it, and learning more. On my way home I kept coming back to that fact: that in a place where I had been an outcast for being trans, there were teenagers proud of their trans friends, fighting their corner, willing to take a stand. There were even teachers ready to do the same.

I didn't know how much pain I had still dragging around behind me until it was set free. It was only with that apology, that experience of making good, that I could feel healing in the places that had scabbed over but never healed. It was somewhat embarrassing – I still expect myself to be invulnerable, in many ways – but I'm so glad that it happened. The nightmares have stopped; after so many years of psychotherapy, my dreams are often obligingly obvious.

It made me realise that those two crucial factors in the happiness or misery of trans people – the support of others, and a sense of engagement in a wider world – are never fixed in place, and the opportunities of both are never over. We try to laugh it off, or decry it bitterly, but we so often think of the pain we've been dealt as a done deal: others have attacked, and we are left with the scars and the necessity to heal ourselves. There is the tendency for some of us trans activists to look at ourselves and say 'we're already damaged goods – we should focus on young people, because at least there's still hope for them'.

I no longer believe that to be true. I don't think it is ever too late for those around us – those who aren't trans – to reach out and offer their support, to make right on where they stumbled and failed. It is incredible what being needed – in both ways – can do. And this is a part of trans liberation that anyone can make good on.

9

Trans/Love

There were two reasons why I was so scared of physical transition, why I vacillated about what it was that I needed, caved in to social pressure; presented myself according to the instructions of others, to the detriment of my mental health and happiness. The first was because I wanted to have a successful career, and I'd never heard of an openly trans classical musician. It seemed an impossibility when I was a teenager. Even now, I only know of a small handful.

The second, more overwhelming concern: that being trans made me unlovable, and that I should keep my body as it was for the sake of someone I couldn't afford to lose.

Trans people occupy a strange place in society when it comes to desirability, sexual attractiveness and our supposed value as romantic partners. In pornography, trans women are highly visible or, rather, *some* trans women are highly visible. The standards for trans women in mainstream porn are no different from other gendered standards in mainstream media: only a narrow band of women are considered worthy.

Otherwise we are, for the most part, invisible or branded as undesirable. In 2016 there were some trans celebrities, a very small number of highly visible and attractive trans women, trans men and genderqueer people. They are outliers. Attraction to a trans person is more usually seen as a joke and a failure. If we match normative standards of what it is to be beautiful then we're deceptive; if we don't we're pathetic. All that we are, all that we could bring to a relationship, is swept away in that judgement: unworthy, repugnant, fake.

I worry that my concerns over appearing desirable, with wanting to be wanted, are a sign of shallowness. I worry that those worries are an inevitable symptom of growing up being told that I was ugly on a daily basis, of being mocked and isolated and told that I deserved it *because* of being ugly. Not feeling at home in my body, it was easy to judge it as a thing apart, and to fear the ways in which it was seen by strangers. I drew graphs, in therapy sessions, of beauty and ugliness, and plotted my own self close to the bottom. I had already read enough feminist theory by that point to know that the beauty myth was harmful, but I also felt, with an iron certainty, that it still applied to me and to my supposed ugliness. I took refuge in what I could do, in how I could think, but it wasn't enough. It was at this juncture that the outer world taught me a crucial lesson to counter my inner knowledge: that I could be wanted, and desired, if I only presented myself in a certain way. At the age of fourteen I was experimenting with my gendered appearance daily; sometimes in flannel and waistcoats, and sometimes in lipstick and high heels. It was one of those times, dressed in feminine clothes, my hair long, my make-up perfect, that an older gentleman leant out of a window in the restaurant we were passing, my family and I, and handed me a flower, because he said I was pretty. It was a pattern that would repeat again and again. In the clothes that made me feel most like myself – my father's old suits, shirts and jeans from the men's section, boots, a scuffed jacket – I was invisible. In dresses and blouses, tight sweaters and padding in a bra, I was desirable: flirted with by strangers, cruised by older women, given little extras in coffee shops and restaurants, told openly and repeatedly 'You're so beautiful'. I didn't feel it – but I so wanted other people to feel it about me.

I think if I had had more time to figure it out on my own it wouldn't have been so hard. Despite that year and a half of confusion, my self-knowledge and self-respect were starting to win through. I found pride in presenting myself in a way that felt congruent with my inner self, in learning the exact things that made me feel happy and at home. I still caved in to outside pressure, particularly when I felt I had something to prove: that I wasn't failing at a standard gendered appearance, I was rejecting it. But then I went to university, fell in love and lost myself in the struggle between what I needed to be and what I needed to do to stay wanted.

It's a terrible truism that the majority of us could look back on our early relationships with regret – I have nothing new to add on that score. I was very far from perfect, and I made a lot of wrong turns and mistakes: I was sorry then, and I'm sorry now.

I was not above reproach in my first major relationship, but neither was I dishonest about my gender, and my fears and hopes of transition. My girlfriend was interested, supportive, in some ways; she read the books that had helped me, bought me gifts that reflected the self I wanted to see. But, at so many other times, there were discrepancies and arguments that we glossed over, which I pretended didn't hurt me. The person she loved wasn't the person I needed to be. She didn't like body hair; after months of pressure, I got rid of mine. The approval of the changes I had made for her worked a magic that requests or complaints could not have achieved. I started wearing skirts, because she thought they were sexy. When my hair was long, she was complimentary; when it was shaved or cut short she withdrew her praise. The day I found a surgeon who was happy to treat me was one of the most exciting of my life; she asked me not to go through with it, because my body as it was made her happy. As she explained, I looked as I wanted to during the day, so why couldn't I stay as she needed me to be when I was naked with her? I loved her in a very young and naïve way – if there had been no other pressures, I suspect our relationship would have ended then, after two and a half years, filled with some wonderful moments but based on a fundamental incompatibility.

What happened instead is hard to write down. My words feel insufficient compared to what I want to say, to the memories I'm trying to describe. I would like to keep what is private, private, and know also that my experience is so typical that it needs to be shared. My brother was diagnosed with a rare and serious form of brain cancer; he was eighteen, I was twenty-one. The odds of survival were not good, with treatments that were unlikely to serve as long-term solutions, but he was young and strong, and determined to try whatever his oncologists suggested. We couldn't hope for a permanent remission, but we could buy time until a treatment that guaranteed remission could be found. We entered those rounds of surgery, chemo and radiotherapy familiar to so many. I clung to my partner, wrote up my degree work in waiting rooms and on trains to and from hospital, and did my best by my brother. The treatments failed, then succeeded, and then the failures began to outweigh the successes. My girlfriend – partner – reaffirmed her commitment to me, to my family, and I leant on her for every ounce of support I could get. She grew more and more uncomfortable with any elements of my appearance that would reflect my transness, my actual gender – and I fell in line. I find it hard, now, to understand just how quickly I acquiesced, how I could be so deeply invested in my transgender self and still be prepared to go against it. I remember one moment of absolute clarity, getting ready for her, facing myself in a full-length mirror. My body was prepped and shaped in all ways to a standard that she would find attractive, from my weight to my pubic hair – and I looked at myself in the mirror, and thought 'How could anyone fail to love *that*?' I no longer felt any connection to my own body as mine. It was just something designed and presented as a bargaining chip, a tool with which to secure another person's desire and care.

I learnt a valuable lesson from that relationship, one I thought I had known but obviously had failed to understand and internalise: if someone loves a certain image of you – an image which misses your true self – then the actuality of who you are will never be enough. No matter how much of myself I cut away to try to reflect back what she wanted to see, I was always found wanting. My brother died just over a year after that memory, and the relationship crumbled soon after that. Bereavement is staggeringly hard, and I was going through with the surgery after all.

*

Contrary to the dire warnings I'd been given – that no one would want me, no one would love me, with my body as it should be and my self recognisable and honest – I found the number of romantic offers I had actually increased. Some were from genuinely wonderful people; I made friends, I went on dates, I kissed a few people I shouldn't have and learnt a lot about myself.

Some of that interest, though, was like an inverted parody of what I had been used to in my teens. Where previously my transness had been undesirable, now it was valuable, but only through a certain reading.

There are some people who say that we shouldn't criticise those cis people who fetishise us: that to do so is to shame someone for something natural and normal. That some attention is better than none at all. What I know is that that particular kind of attention made my skin crawl, and left me feeling almost as misread as the people who had wanted me to hide who I was. There were so many innuendos, assumptions, questions about my genitals. I was told that I was the 'best of both worlds', told that my masculinity was so much more attractive than a cis man's, because I was 'special', because I was different, because I was exotic and strange. Cis people asked me to be their 'first'. They grabbed me, and pressured me, and one particular man with a crush insisted on touching my chest so as to publicly announce whether I felt 'real' or not. They fixated on their own ideas of what being trans meant to the exclusion of the reality of the trans person in front of them. It was another way of being objectified, of being reduced to a shell and a foreign narrative. I had just begun to come into a sense of comfort in my body, a deliberate attempt to learn how to care for myself, and I found that being alone was preferable to being wanted for what I am not.

What I've learnt about love and desire and ways of seeing is not limited to interactions between cis and trans people. Neither is it indicative of all such interactions; cis and trans are blunt words for societal categories and prescriptions, and there are many, many people who stretch beyond their bounds in all areas of life. But I think there are common patterns, trends, that come from a meeting between a person naturalised in the belief that they are natural, and a person who has learnt that what is natural for them is wrong, strange and subject to the approval of others. From so many of the people I have met and known, desired and been desired by, I have learnt that a trans person's needs, reality and physicality are supposed to be secondary to those of a cis person. I've learnt it from the chasers who pursued me with specific ideas about how and when I should fuck them, regardless of how little interest I expressed. It was taught to me by a boyfriend who flipped between loving me and pushing me away, accepting my androgyny and sighing 'You would have made a beautiful woman'. It's the message I received from men and women, gay and straight, who have admitted their attraction and followed it with 'you confuse me' – not that these people are confused, but that I am responsible for their confusion.

What I have also learnt, in time, is that there is nothing inevitable about this pattern, and no excuses for it. That was a lesson that came slowly: through meeting other trans people, caring for other trans people, being taught through the care of others to care for myself – through losing my brother and my partner at the same time and realising that it was possible to go on alone. Through being loved conditionally, and learning that it's never enough. And, finally, through being loved unconditionally, and realising the utter difference between the two.

It's the difference between making love to the person you love with yourself presented as a character in an artificial scene you hope will please them – withdrawing from your own body into a dislocated fantasy – and fucking so truthfully, in a way that is so totally in the moment, that the body is full to overflowing with a sense of total peace. It's the distance between a desperation to be found beautiful and the knowledge that the whole of who I am *is* beautiful to my partner, and 'beautiful' in a way that goes deeper than my appearance. It's the change between pursuing the approval of the loved one as someone desired – known but also distant – and finding your best friend standing at your side.

It might seem a small thing to be angry about, compared with the overt hatred, workplace discrimination, denial of health care and education, but it's an anger that hits deep. I cannot believe that, for so long, despite my best efforts to believe in my self, I so fully capitulated to the idea that the full expression of my true self was unworthy of care.

It doesn't have to be this way. There is no reason for it to be so.

If we are to be treated with respect in the wider world, we must trust in the respect of those closest to us. The micro and the macro are inseparable. Trans people are worthy of love.

10

Are Trans People Real?

Proving that we are *really* trans is only the first hurdle. Being 'trans' is the diagnostic, the category we are placed in or place ourselves in in order to make sense of the bigger, deeper truth we are telling: that some of us are men, and some of us are women, and some of us are none of the above, but that we are really, truly these things despite the categorisation of our bodies by others at birth. When it comes to the genuine nature of our genders, it is clear that many people might recognise the fact that we're transgender, but never grant us the status of 'real' men and 'real' women, to say nothing of the rest.

We, as trans people, are held up as fakes in contrast to the cis original. The words 'parody' and 'pantomime' come up a lot. Germaine Greer's 2007 book *The Whole Woman* contains a chapter on trans and intersex people titled 'Pantomime Dames'. Richard Littlejohn (again) refers to us as 'the "trans" pantomime'.

The idea that trans women are fake women, that trans men

are fake men, is one that is currently playing out in schools, prisons, the legal system, public life, the political circus that inflames every other arena. It is an issue frequently dismissed as a simple difference of opinions, characterised by the 'right to offend' – but it is no exaggeration to say that, at its worst, this question of realness can mean life or death to the most vulnerable members of our community.

Nowhere is the fight over trans realness as openly vicious as in the current battle over access to public toilets, public changing rooms and public life. What began as a small fringe concern – the dawning realisation that trans people exist, and need to use gendered facilities just like everyone else – has stormed front and centre into the mainstream political debate. In America, North Carolina passed its anti-trans bathroom bill in 2016. The Republican National Committee approved a resolution endorsing similar bathroom bills soon after; current president Donald Trump flip-flopped on the issue, before capitulating to popular anti-trans sentiment. Ted Cruz seemed to think he had hit on a solution, proposing that trans people only be allowed to use the bathrooms in their own homes. Cruel, but better than the proposal of the Rowan-Salisbury Board of Education, which voted to allow students to carry pepper spray in case of attack by trans bathroom predators – a decision later repealed after widespread condemnation. Online news stories feature everyday Americans proud to announce the fact that they'll be carrying guns into public bathrooms to fend off trans people; megastore Target has been under attack for their decision to allow trans people to use the bathrooms that best match our genders.

Proponents of these laws – bills that would force people to use the bathrooms associated with the original indicated on a birth certificate, rather than with their lived gender – are keen on the generalities, and not so clear on specifics. How are these laws to be enforced? The assumption is, I suppose, that trans people are easy to spot. It's certainly true that some trans people look nothing like the stereotypes surrounding the sex they were assigned at birth. It's also very clear to see that many people, cis and trans, do not fit gender normative standards of appearance. What happens when there's confusion: does it come down to a majority opinion? Driver's licence, passport, ID cards? All of those documents can be updated without doing the same to a birth certificate. A physical pat-down by a security guard? How the hell is that meant to play out with children and teenagers? These bills are a logical, logistical, ethical mess, and they're playing well with a sizeable subset of the population.

I wonder at how quickly we've forgotten the similar arguments made over bisexual and gay people having access to 'normal' bathrooms and changing rooms. They were extremely popular when I was growing up, trotted out as the number one reason why LGB people should not serve in the army, play mainstream sports, be allowed to come out at school, be allowed to teach in schools, be allowed to *attend* regular schools. This was the era of Section 28: an amendment brought in under Margaret Thatcher's government banning the teaching of 'the acceptability of homosexuality as a pretended family relationship'. As a teenager, the supposed danger of gay and bisexual people was a regular topic of school debate; the majority consensus was that any teacher suspected of being gay shouldn't be allowed alone in a room with pupils, and certainly shouldn't be allowed to supervise them in PE. I felt the pressure of it, when we were changing before and after sports lessons, and was shocked by the number of straight people who assumed that every queer person was just someone waiting for the right opportunity.

Now that the gay rights movement has spread into the mainstream, and these horrible predications have failed to come true, that need to scapegoat has shifted over onto trans people. The myth of the trans predator has made it into several campaign videos: hairy, hulking, monstrous, this figure has more in common with Bigfoot than any actual trans person. It's a genuine urban legend for our time. Politicians in favour of these bills paint trans people (particularly trans women), trans children, as conniving sexual suspects. Twice-disappointed presidential hopeful Mike Huckabee came out against allowing trans people equal access to restrooms and changing rooms with the line that, had he known about trans people when he was growing up, he would have pretended to be trans in order to watch the girls shower after gym class.

How did it ever come to this? Given the force of the reaction, one could be forgiven for thinking this panic, this clampdown, is the fallout from the actions of a trans criminal using public bathrooms to prey on women and children.

But no. As far as I am aware – and at the time of writing this – there has not been a single reported case of a trans person attacking a cis person in a public bathroom. Ever.

Public toilets are, however, common settings for transphobic violence. They're common settings for violence, full stop. I know several cis women who have been raped by cis men in public toilets; the glyph on the door does nothing to stop an actual predator. Cis men beat up other cis men in the toilets all the time. If we want to tackle violence and abuse, and God knows we should, then we should be telling these stories and learning from them, rather than investing in the myth that public toilets are safe so long as we keep the trans people out. As ever, trans people are held to a totally different standard; our access to basic services can be denied or granted depending on perceived, even imaginary, good or bad behaviour.

Cutting off access to public bathrooms cuts off access to public life. You can't move through the world, can't use public transport, can't hold down a job, can't go to school, can't visit a hospital, without using the bathroom. I have OCD and a fear of germs, so trust me on this one – I tried. All that happened was that I made myself ill through drinking less than half a litre of water a day. When I was first coming out into the trans community in London, I heard other people joke about 'trans bladder syndrome', the fact that we were so used to holding it in that we could go for staggering lengths of time without using a bathroom, often resulting in a urinary tract infection. For someone like me, whose gendered appearance is judged in different ways by different people, picking the 'right' bathroom to use is a constant struggle. I've been turned away from both men's and women's restrooms, and accepted in both. Occasionally, the comments are endearing: a small child whispering loudly, 'Mummy, why is that man wearing make-up?' Mostly, the stares are off-putting, and I make it a point never to use a restroom where it seems like the reaction would be worse than stares or embarrassed exclamations. I have no idea what I'd do if it was decided that I had to use the bathroom that matched my birth certificate. For many trans people, what these laws mean are women in men's rooms and men in the ladies' rooms, the very thing these rulings claim to oppose. Enforcing these laws will inevitably mean an upsurge in violence, people victimised and hurt for having the audacity to have human bodily functions. These politicians pretend to want a crackdown on such violence. It seems to me that they're more than happy to see an increase in it – so long as the victims are trans.

A trans woman is locked up in a men's prison – can you guess the rest? She's told that it's her own fault, that she brought it on herself; she should perform sexual acts to try to keep herself safe: she should resign herself to being raped, over and over again. Her face will be sliced open with a razor. She has no right to say no.

That's what happened to Passion Star, a Texan trans woman, for over a decade. Here is what happened to twenty-one-year-old Vicky Thompson in 2015: despite her fragile mental state, despite her pleas to serve her time in a women's prison, she was sent to HMP Leeds, despite her boyfriend warning the prison that she would kill herself in a men's jail. She was found dead in her cell a week later. These stories pour in from around the world and coalesce into marked patterns: a vulnerable trans woman, most often a woman of colour, a migrant woman, a poor woman, a sex worker – maybe some or all of these things – is arrested. She is often held without trial. She is frequently failed by her court-appointed lawyer. She is sentenced and sent to a men's prison, and there she is abused by the staff or by the inmates or by both. She is sexually harassed; she is usually raped. In some instances she is denied her medication; or she is denied any health care at all. If she complains, she may be punished:

put into solitary confinement 'for her own protection'. Sometimes, she will take a plea bargain to escape; sometimes, she will take her own life. Chelsea Manning, the US Army whistleblower currently serving a thirty-five-year sentence in a men's military prison, (having only publically come out the day after her sentencing) recently attempted suicide. In the six years following her initial arrest she was held, on and off, in solitary confinement, denied her hormones and denied the right to present herself in a feminine way. Her desperation should have come as no surprise. Following a widely-publicised hunger strike, the army's position appeared to change: Manning was promised a chance at medical transition. Her sentence commuted by President Obama, Chelsea Manning is now a free woman: thousands of trans prisoners around the world will have no such escape.

In the UK, the Ministry of Justice claims that the majority of trans prisoners will be held in a prison that matches their lived gender; there are guidelines and internal rules. Trans prisoners have the right to continue medical treatment, the right to be detained without fear of emotional abuse and violence. Whether those rights are respected remains to be seen. Trans prisoners with a Gender Recognition Certificate (GRC) should be automatically placed in the correct prison; however, the majority of trans people in the UK do not have a GRC, as they are difficult and costly to obtain. GRCs are only available to trans people who have completed a standard medical transition, who have gathered the evidence of their doctors, paid a fee and had this evidence accepted by an anonymous Gender Recognition Panel. Many trans people have their evidence dismissed, some of us are disqualified from the get-go, and most don't see the point in trying.

Opponents claim that they don't want to see trans women – or, in their words, men – suffer: they simply don't want to see cis women, *real* women, under threat. The myth of the predator is absolute. Lack of evidence is ignored, the rape of cis women by cis women in prison is ignored, broader questions of prisoners' rights are ignored. Deeper concerns – how can this be called justice? How many other prisoners suffer? – are glossed over. What matters here is an appearance of law and order, the appearance of punishment, the appearance of safety. Once someone has been locked away, the reality can be forgotten.

There are people who say that trans women lose their right to be treated as women the minute they commit a crime. They claim that women are, by nature, more peaceful than men, not driven to violence, and that, by being arrested, a trans woman has exiled herself from a category she had no right to claim.

In the absolute worst cases of denying the authenticity of trans genders, we find a toxic mix of transphobia, misogyny and homophobia known as the trans panic defence. People who claim this defence try to excuse their behaviour thus: that finding out that someone, usually a woman, is trans sparks a feeling of disgust, fear and rage so strong that the perpetrator of any subsequent crime can be excused their actions. To exist at all, this idea has to play on cruel and incorrect ideas of what it is to be trans, what it is to be a woman, and what it is to be straight or gay. Let me be very clear: trans women are women, and it does not make a straight cis man gay to be attracted to a woman. But the way trans panic plays out – in just one of its erasures and attacks – is in a cis man's fear that he will be considered queer, because the woman he's attracted to was assigned male at birth.

The trans panic response can be found in all kinds of places. *The Crying Game*, Neil Jordan's 1992 movie, depicts a classic example of type. Fergus, our anti-hero, discovers that the woman he's involved with, Dil, is trans; he hits her and rushes to the toilet to vomit. You can find similar reaction sequences in movies and TV shows throughout the nineties and 2000s. Sometimes it's played for tragedy, sometimes for titillation, and sometimes just for laughs.

It's a trope that's been used so often that *Family Guy*, infamous for its need to be more shocking than shocking, had to find a way of outdoing the standard. In the 2010 episode 'Quagmire's Dad', they did this by having one of their main characters sleep with a trans woman, and then vomit for thirty seconds straight on learning her trans status, later referring to her as a man. In response to criticism from LGBT and feminist groups, creator Seth MacFarlane claimed, 'It's probably the most sympathetic portrayal of a transexual [sic] character that has ever been on television.' MacFarlane later double-downed on his comments, explaining the necessity of all that vomit with: 'If I found out that I had slept with a transsexual, I might throw up in the same way that a gay guy looks at a vagina and goes, "Oh, my God, that's disgusting".'

I find this idea of the necessity of vomiting a fascinating, albeit depressing, one. I've made out with people whom I didn't find attractive, but it's never made me sick. I've also been turned on by people I didn't particularly like, people I didn't want to go any further with and, again, no vomiting, nor any desire to publicly express how sick they'd supposedly made me. It wasn't anyone's *fault*, least of all theirs, that we weren't compatible, and I had nothing to prove. In this trans panic trope, vomiting is a public sign of disgust, a signal to cancel out what would have been implied by a kiss, a caress, an erection. This isn't about trans women being disgusting, and it isn't about straight men being disgusted *by* trans women. This is about safety, proof, social status and the performance of a narrow idea of straight masculinity.

The public nature of avenging an insult is all too apparent in the behaviour of the contestants of a 2004 reality dating show, *There's Something About Miriam*. The format was pretty standard – six young men competed for the attentions of a beautiful Mexican model – the 'twist' being that she was trans. Tom Rooke, the winner, initially accepted the prize of £10,000 and a holiday with Miriam; later, he and the other contestants filed a lawsuit against the makers of the programme. They alleged conspiracy to commit sexual assault, defamation, breach of contract, and personal injury in the form of psychological and emotional damage. Apparently, being attracted to a trans woman is dangerous enough to warrant not only a public disavowal, but also legal action. The company settled out of court for an undisclosed sum. The plaintiffs had successfully performed their disgust, no matter the fact of their initial attraction.

What plays out in the media as comedy or drama is enacted in real life as tragedy, with legal systems only too happy to play the trans panic card. The victims of violence are painted as revolting, disposable, and deceptive, blamed for their own deaths. Their killers are absolved of all responsibility: in this interpretation exterminating a threat like that is something that could happen to anyone.

One of the most famous of these cases was that of Californian teenager Gwen Araujo, murdered at party in 2002 by two former lovers and their friends. Her genitals were forcibly inspected; one ex-lover vomited. She was subjected to extreme and extended violence, taken into the garage and murdered. Her body was dumped in the Sierra Nevada mountains; her killers, when caught, when tried, claimed that their actions were the result of Gwen's trans status. They were found guilty, but of second-degree murder and voluntary manslaughter – lesser convictions – and without the additional weight of hate crime legislation.

The murders of trans women, of trans feminine people, who are 'discovered' are often marked by their appalling brutality. Very often there was no 'discovery' at all: the popularity of trans panic trope just makes for an easy excuse for transmisogynistic killers. Speaking to *VICE* magazine in 2016, Turkish trans woman Olya had this to say about the constant threat such men pose: '"My friend was killed and the murderer is still out there. He could be my next client. But I still have to work. In this community, nobody ever dies of natural causes. Every day, I come back home from work, shut the door behind myself, and take a deep breath and say, "Thank God I'm alive for one more day" … People who demand to have sex with transgender women tend to be those behind the murders. Sometimes, after having sex, they feel embarrassed about having slept with a transgender woman … It doesn't suit their manliness. They get aggressive and kill the sex worker."'

Some advocates, commentators and organisations have declared an epidemic of violence against trans women, nearly always trans women of colour, poor trans women, women in sex work. Speaking to *Vox*, Chase Strangio of the ACLU explains: 'The bodies of trans women of color are the site of multiple forms of deeply historical oppression. That's a critical part of understanding the violence against trans people.'

That trans panic is used as a defence by people who target marginalised trans women does not give us a convenient, simplistic explanation for this wave of violence. It is one thread in a broader story of dehumanisation and oppression. Author, broadcaster and trans pioneer Janet Mock has been tireless in underlining the fact that the violence faced by trans women is not single-sourced, but a deadly combination of prejudices, the result of multiple marginalisations. Speaking on MSNBC in 2015, Mock stated:

> These women are more that just a compilation of names and ages and stories of violence and trauma. They were people. People living at a vulnerable intersection of race, gender, and class. People existing in a culture where they fell in between the cracks of racial justice, feminist, and LGBT movements. People whose names are only spoken by the majority of us when they can no longer respond … Today we learn their stories and say their names, not out of obligation, but out of recognition that these 17 women had value, had purposes, and were loved. And they will be missed.

And then there are headlines like these:

'Woman who used fake penis to have sex with a woman avoids jail'

'Woman duped by lesbian with fake penis reveals her horror'

'Lincolnshire woman posed as man and sexually assaulted woman she met on Facebook'

In December 2015 the case of Kyran Lee, a trans man, and an unnamed woman who accused him of assault by deception, hit the news. The case itself is confusing, unnerving, the reporting of it appalling. The facts: Lee, going by the name of Joey, began a relationship with a woman, which developed in the usual kind of way. They sent each other messages, they spent the night together, they had phone sex. The woman, Lee's lawyer claims, gave Lee a sexual ultimatum: that they would consummate the relationship, or it was over. Lee, who had not yet begun medical transition, used a prosthetic – pretty standard practice for many trans masculine people. His partner described the experience as normal. Later, she was told of Lee's birth name, the fact that he was trans; she went to the police and reported him for assault – not because she had not consented, but because she would not have consented if she knew the sex he was assigned at birth. Lee was arrested and recorded as a woman: later acceptance of the fact that he is a trans man seems to have had no retroactive effect, and did not alter the arguing of or judgement on the case. The presiding judge, Michael Heath, described Lee's desire to have a relationship as 'selfish ... dreadful and deceitful'. He recognised that Kryan Lee was a trans man, albeit in a way that many trans people found inaccurate, but imposed a two-year suspended prison sentence, and said that he would have sent Lee straight to prison if he believed his motives to have been sexual in nature.

There is so much to unpack here, and so much that feels as though it can't be solved. At what point does a trans person become their 'real' gender? After a certain amount of medical treatment? After a certain amount of time? There is confusion over 'how trans' Lee knew himself to be at the time of the incident – but is there a cut-off point? Are trans people only trans from the moment they announce themselves publicly? It certainly looks as though the police, the courts and the media all believe that a trans man is really a woman, if his medical transition is still in its early stages. Not only that, but that there are legal limits to presenting yourself *as you are*, if you do so without informing others that your standards of realness and their standards of realness may differ. What counts as 'real' when it comes to the body? The verdict was unanimous in this case: a prosthetic penis is a 'fake' penis, it cannot be substituted for the 'real' thing. But is this the case with all prostheses, or only some? Would a prosthetic be allowed when used by a cis man? Is it the penis itself, or the ultimately 'fake' body of a trans man that's seen as illegitimate? Are there set rules, or are we making this up as we go along?

I believe in informed consent. I believe in sex with honesty as its foundation. I believe that every individual has the right to decide what is happening to their body and who it's happening with. But what I don't understand, in this case and others like it, is what counts as deception, and why some kinds of deception are punishable in a court of law, and others are key elements of our sexual culture.

Imagine if the last time you slept with your boyfriend, you did so with the (supposed) knowledge that you were monogamous, that you had both been screened for STIs, that you were able to have sex without barrier protection, and that he was supportive of your transition. Then he tells you, after a night of unprotected sex, that he had been sleeping around without using condoms, had got someone pregnant, hadn't been tested, didn't want to be with you any longer, didn't want to be with a trans person – but could he keep having sex with you until he found someone better? It's not an unusual story, and neither is the one where you then wait anxiously for your test results, hating yourself for having been so trusting. Would you at any point think of going to the police and pushing an assault by deception charge?

There are so many ways a person can be damaged through sex and deception. I'm not trying to make light of any of them. Even when I deplore the transphobia behind cases like Kyran Lee's, I feel for anyone who feels as though their consent was given without knowing all that they wanted, or needed, to know. But I distrust the fact that the government, and the courts, have decided that some deceptions are not deceptions, and some 'deceptions' are criminal. If it were to do with actual harm caused, the cases would overrun the courts. As it stands, 'sex by deception' seems to be all about policing the line between those whose gender is acceptable to the state and those whose gender isn't – and punishing those who don't make the grade for having the audacity to present themselves as real.

So many problems come down to a trans person not having the right identification, lacking the updated birth certificate, driver's licence or passport that shows them in their true gender. The responsibility passes back to each individual trans person; the law has given us recognition, and if we can't match the law's requirements, if we get into trouble before we've seen to our paperwork, then the law is absolved of responsibility, instead of believing what we say.

I wonder what the kind of person who believes that thinks happens when you socially transition. That it's as easy as filling in a form? Or that the Kafkaesque struggles with the legal and medical systems are justified, to make sure the process weeds out any trans people who aren't real enough to be counted?

Depending on the country, these are some of the ways in which we are required to earn our realness: sterilisation, divorce, institutionalisation, disowning our families (or never having had them), and by conforming to strict and unbending stereotypes of what a man or a woman should be in appearance, sexuality, beliefs and habits. In many countries – France, for example – an individual must petition the courts for a change of name and gender; the decision will come down to the opinion of a single judge. So far, only a tiny number of countries accept the existence of genders beyond female or male. In the UK, you must amass a case of 'evidence' including doctors' reports, proof that you've completed a standard medical transition, or acceptable excuses as to why you haven't. That evidence goes before a panel of strangers, a verdict is given; if they reject an application it may be several years before a person can apply again.

There are ways of doing it differently. Malta, Argentina, Denmark, Norway and Ireland have decided that self-determination is enough, that all a trans person needs to do to be real is to declare it in an official form. So far, there have been no problems. The idea there would be problems is laughable. Trans people are living their real lives, with or without government protection.

If not through official channels how do we, then, find and declare who we know ourselves to be: men, women, beyond the binary?

Being trans, being in community with other trans people, has taught me a great deal. This experience, of what it is to find authenticity, has been one of the most profound.

I've seen it expressed, tested, confirmed by poets on makeshift stages, their make-up glowing in the spotlights, their bodies and clothes a handcrafted model of self-expression. I've heard it in the voices of other singers – basses to sopranos of all and no genders – the voice as an instrument and a conduit of a message. Seen it simply in the way bodies relax around each other, knowing that there is no judgement – express themselves with shyness or extravagance, but with that incredible sense of intimacy – that three o'clock in the morning feeling, when everyone is vulnerable in what they say, and everyone is reckless with that vulnerability. Novels, autobiography, history, theory: each form stripping a layer away. Learning a new way of language with every individual story, in the same way as learning the unique timbre of a voice, the formation of letters, the percussion of breath. Being taught that each form of physical presence – skin, clothes, hair, flesh – will have its own interpretation and way of resisting interpretation. That we can be more than we were taught we could be. That what other people say about us does not translate into who we are. That there are many different paths to happiness, and even more ways in which to travel them.

I had, and most likely still have, a tendency towards didacticism. It made me feel superior, when most of my world told me I was wrong. I am so thankful to all the people who have helped me to unlearn the defence of believing my particular truth to be universal. They taught me to really listen to other people, and to accept the limits of my own knowledge. I have never really liked putting my self into words. Listening taught me that the labels that confined me could liberate others. That the right answer for one person could become the wrong answer for another, and that all we could do was lend support in our shared individuality.

The other side of that practice, of course, was learning to truly embrace my own right answers, without imposing artificial limits on what I could learn or seeking approval for my findings.

These ways of questioning, knowing and being are some of the greatest rewards of the trans experience. When asked if I could turn back the clock and live my life as a cis person, it's these experiences that I hold onto as the reason why I wouldn't take that option. They're ones I wish I could share more widely. We all invest so much in fighting the fear of being found wanting. Advertising, fashion, cosmetics, self-help, magazines, television, weight-loss industries – all of them promise to reveal the 'real' us if we buy what they're selling and change who we are. Anxiety sells. Fear of loneliness sells. Fear of mockery, of social failure, sells so very well. We are encouraged to ascribe to singular philosophies, join a group, and find ourselves a bulwark against the world. If we buy the right thing, do the right thing, become the correct forms of our gendered selves, then maybe we'll be safe, desirable, powerful, loved.

I wonder if this is one of the reasons why some people hate trans people with such a passion, wanting not just to stamp us out but to erase all signs of our transgressions. Not because we have failed at trying to live by society's gendered rules, but because we have broken these rules and still found happiness. We have learnt to make our own gendered standards, and in so doing have found desire, love, power. Not having the safety of wider society, we have built places of safety for each other. Not seeing ourselves reflected in the outside world, we have learnt how to trust in each other's reflections.

Trans people are far from being the only people to have learnt how to find an unrecognised, liberating truth, in defiance of the pressure to court sameness and conformity. But that truth – something intrinsic to the self – is one I have learnt from my trans siblings, and one I have heard celebrated over and over again throughout our communities.

I wouldn't wish the pain of dysphoria, or the weight of transphobic oppression, on anyone, but still – I wish there was a way that I could share the kind of peace that comes after years of relentless questioning. There is the tendency for some cis people to believe that being trans is about fixing some kind of defect, that we have to alter our 'transgendered' selves in order to slot back into place into a gendered society bound about by struggle and by rules.

For myself, I think it could be the other way around.

11

The Denial of History

A quarter of the way through *The Danish Girl* I was just about ready to get to my feet and give the late-night audience my best Hermione Granger impression. I was tired, angry and sick of seeing the same old story play out on the screen in front of me. Admittedly, I had not gone in with high expectations: responses from trans audiences had been extremely poor, and friends had warned me not to expect too much. I had read part of the script already and, as someone fascinated by the period of history during which the film is set, was horrified by the factual inaccuracies I saw. Still, in my defence, I had hoped for the best and, after a long day teaching and given the price of the ticket, I wanted to enjoy myself.

It was not to be. This being London, I squashed the desire to lecture those around me on what *really* happened, and settled for scribbling furiously in my notebook, cringing every time the audience laughed at Eddie Redmayne's attempts to present himself as a woman.

Visually, dramatically – even orchestrally – similar to

Tom Hooper's previous award-winner *The King's Speech*, *The Danish Girl* was a strange experience for me. A 'based on a true story' biopic, drawn from the book of the same name, it purports to loosely tell the story of Danish painter Einar Wegener, wife and fellow artist Gerda Wegener, and the woman Einar reveals herself to be: the beautiful and ill-fated Lili Elbe. The film itself is gorgeous, of course, with that lush yet muted aesthetic that screams 'classy period piece': *Downton Abbey* on a bigger budget. Everything, from the restrained and unobtrusive directorial style, to the pre-credit reminder that the diary Lili is shown writing was turned into a memoir, points to the telling of an underlying truth. The marketing – posters, puff pieces, interviews with the actors – makes it explicit: here is a real life story of a transgender pioneer, and what you're about to see next will shock and amaze you. Failing to support this film is failing to support trans history, trans visibility and trans acceptance.

But the problem is, is that what this film is passing off as 'real life' is nothing more than a collection of stories, based on a myth of trans victimhood and suffering at odds with the real life of Lili Elbe and her peers.

The basic facts: before Lili Elbe was known as Lili Elbe, she was known as Einar Wegener. Born in 1882 and trained at the Royal Danish Academy of Fine Arts, she married Gerda Gottlieb in 1904, while both of them were still students. As painters, both Einar and Gerda enjoyed some initial success, with Gerda's career quickly outstripping her partner's. They moved to Paris, they moved back to Copenhagen, they loved and supported each other, and eventually parted ways to pursue other marriages, remaining close and loving friends.

What makes their story of interest to outsiders, of course, is the fact that Lili became posthumously famous as one of the first people to pursue a surgical transition. She died in 1931, two months on from her fourth (or possibly fifth) and final operation, a uterine transplant. *Man Into Woman* appeared in 1933, and Lili's name was made. While touting itself as a memoir, *Man Into Woman* was actually written by Danish journalist Loulou Lassen and German writer Ernst Jacobson, who took the pseudonym Niels Hoyer and title of editor. Jacobson fleshed out his third-person narrative with extracts from Lili's letters and diary entries. Nerissa Gailey and AD Brown explain, in their 2015 essay 'Beyond Either/or', the many ways in which *Man Into Woman* is closer to fiction than fact: discrepancies between the book and the original documents it refers to, lack of verification of its contents due to the destruction of records in the fire-bombing of Dresden, and the number of alterations and exaggerations found throughout the text.

Information about Lili and Gerda can be found in a scattering of sources: contemporary accounts written in trans(vestite) magazines, academic papers that have collated and analysed medical accounts, wider media accounts and papers left by the pair. There are many aspects of their shared life that we cannot know and can't guess at. What we do know, though, is at odds with how *The Danish Girl* presents the world.

There are the general problems with the biopic format, and this film was based on a book which itself only claimed to be loosely inspired by Lili's story. Perhaps we could shrug these differences off as a necessary aspect of artistic licence. The compression of years to create a tightened narrative, for example, is standard Hollywood practice. But when the topic – transition – is relatively unknown, these standard practices introduce troubling inaccuracies and distortions. The shortening of timescale makes a gradual realisation and multistaged, multifaceted transition look like some kind of overnight fancy. It may be easier on the audience's attention span, but it props up the popular myth that trans people transition on a whim. There are the usual insertions of fictional characters, some clichéd writing and some heavy-handed pathetic fallacy; par for the course, but aggravatingly faithful to the usual trans tropes. But, beyond these features, there are four specific changes made to Lili and Gerda's story that I just couldn't get my head around, changes that felt so regressive, so oppositional to what actually happened, that it made me wonder what the filmmakers were trying to say about women in general, and being a trans woman in particular.

One of the most shocking moments of the film, one most likely to garner the sympathies of a general audience, is the point at which Lili first seeks help for her 'problem', and is forcibly strapped down and subjected to a radiotherapy cure meant to restore her to a state of normal manhood. Gerda is present to encourage her, to enforce the idea that this painful, excessive response is what's right, is what's needed to save their marriage. The cure fails, of course, but leaves Lili wary of seeking help. In reality, the radiotherapy treatment Lili undertook – with the full support of Gerda – was designed to stimulate the ovaries doctors suspected her of having. Radiotherapy, as a new and exciting development in the field of medicine, was often touted as a revitalising cure-all. In this instance, it was thought that the beams would kick-start ovarian function and that a natural bodily transition would follow. Lili began to bleed on a monthly basis afterwards, and both she and Gerda felt this akin to menstruation, a sign that the treatment was working.

Returning to the movie: following the failure of radiation treatment, Lili shutters herself away, unable to trust to doctors, unable to confide in Gerda and unable to withstand public scrutiny as either Lili or Einar. There is no mention here of Lili's actual life: her consultations and treatments with Magnus Hirschfeld's Institute, her (supposed) disdain for the other patients, her first operation, her love of walking through Paris while drinking life in. Lili does, admittedly, go for a Parisian stroll in *The Danish Girl*, only to be assaulted by two strangers – another invention. Where in reality we have a single trans person as one of many – a pioneer, to be sure, but a pioneer in community – we are shown instead a lone martyr. She becomes someone who cannot be understood, who cannot seek understanding or companionship, who cannot find release even in the solitary pleasures of anonymity.

Lili's final operations and death scene are, inevitably, played for maximum effect. All trace of Hirschfeld erased, Lili and Gerda try a last-ditch consultation with maverick surgeon Kurt Warnekros. He warns them how dangerous his proposed treatment would be. He tells them that Lili would be the first to try. Lili doesn't care; she needs surgery more than the security of a long life. The surgery undertaken is reduced to two procedures, from the likely four or five the real-life Lili underwent: first, the removal of original tissue and, second, the creation of a vagina. Lili is meant to rest properly between procedures, get her strength back– she doesn't. Asking her surgeon if she'll be able to have children after her second operation, she gets the patronising reply: 'One thing at a time'. You can guess the rest. Gerda conveniently arrives at just the right moment for the big death scene, caused by loss of blood and post-surgical fever, and

Lili gets in a final, saccharine line before the delicate closing of her eyes. Gerda cries. The audience, presumably, cries. Lili pays the ultimate price for trying to go against nature – but wasn't she brave to do so?

The reality is far less operatic. The details are somewhat murky, after the destruction of medical records by both the Nazis and by Allied fire-bombing. What we know is that Lili wanted children, and that Warnekros was less ethical than the more cautious, and qualified, Hirschfeld. Successful organ transplants would not become a reality until the production of powerful immunosuppressive drugs in the 1970s. The insurmountable problem of rejection was well known in medicine by the point of Lili's final operation, but Warnekros told her he could do it. Her immune system rejected the transplant – she died on 13 September 1931.

It surprised me, then, that the cinematic change that made me even angrier than this melodramatic surgery and death sequence was the overall treatment of Gerda. Gerda Wegener – whose income from her art outstripped her partner's by a considerable amount, who won two gold medals for her work at the 1925 World's Fair in Paris, who had lived in Paris since 1912 with Lili as two women together, who funded the majority of Lili's surgery, whose best works are some of the most romantic and erotic depictions of lesbian attraction and of lesbian love-making I have ever seen – is reduced and changed to become a character straight out of central casting. Gerda's career only lifts off with Lili's transition, and she becomes, by turn, frustrated, angry and shrewish about the loss of her husband. Gone is any attempt to accurately portray the Bohemian world of independent women, artistic freedom and gendered authenticity, replaced instead by a portrait of a marriage ruined by transition, identical to every other telling of that story from HBO's *Normal* to the join-the-dots tabloid staple. Some, but by no means all, marriages do falter in the face of transition. But attempting to impose that story onto the real lives of Gerda Wegener and Lili Elbe is an insult to how they lived, how they loved, their courage and their artistry. Alicia Vikander brought home the Oscar for Best Supporting Actress: another remarkable chapter of women's history publicly erased.

I was ranting about all of this online – I try, but I'm only human – and I had an interesting response from an ex-pupil of mine. She commented that it wasn't the film's fault that it was so tragic, because that's simply what life was like for trans people in the 1920s. I don't blame her for thinking so: it's what I thought, before I fell down the rabbit hole of historical research. We're still struggling for LGBT acceptance now, so it makes sense that the situation would be much worse nearly a century ago.

Without doubt, tragedy existed, and many, many people suffered. But the story is not quite so bleak as *The Danish Girl* would have you believe. Sometimes, it even manages to be quite wonderful.

It's difficult to pinpoint where to begin – with the birth of the science of sexology in the nineteenth century? With the ball, bar and party scenes in Paris, in Holland, in Berlin, where dancers could present themselves as any gender they liked and flirt with whomever they chose, twice a week in Berlin with police permission. Maybe with the 1882 case of Herman Karl, previously known as Sophia Hedwig, who, after chest and genital surgery, was granted a legal change of name and gender by the Prussian state?

Or maybe with the fact that people who flouted gendered conventions, who insisted on determining their own
gendered selves in opposition to how the world categorised
them, were so well-documented that contemporaneous
researchers could argue over whose definition best described
them. In addition to the words 'transvestite' (a much broader
term, closer to 'transgender' now) and 'transsexual' (appearing in the 1920s), we had 'eviration' and 'defemination'
from Richard von Krafft-Ebing, *Geschlechtsumwandlungstreib*
(drive for sex transformation) from Max Marcuse, and 'Sexo-
Aesthetic Inversion' from Havelock Ellis – in addition to the
complex and conflicting meanings of 'invert', 'Urning', and
'homosexual'. It was Magnus Hirschfeld's words – transvestite and transsexual – that stuck, and Hirschfeld's work that
is behind so many of the extraordinary medical and societal
advances that paved the way for the modern trans movement
today.

A doctor, researcher and all-round campaigner for the
rights of sexual and gendered minorities, Magnus Hirschfeld
was described by Adolf Hitler as 'the most dangerous Jew in
Germany'. In 1897 he founded the Scientific-Humanitarian
Committee, most likely the first campaigning group for what
we would call LGBT causes in the world. He published
a journal, *Yearbook for Sexual Intermediaries*, featuring scientific studies, news, reviews, letters and pictures. In 1919
he founded the Institute for Sexual Science in Berlin, and
in 1928 he founded the World League for Sexual Reform.
In between treating patients, acting as an expert witness,
petitioning the police and the courts for fairer treatment and
writing and distributing political and informational pamphlets, Hirschfeld found the time to write and publish his

groundbreaking book *Transvestites* in 1910. Hirschfeld used the word to describe those who felt 'peace, security and exaltation, happiness and well-being' when presenting as the sex other than which they were assigned at birth – and made it clear that such people could come from all walks of life, could be assigned female or male, could be of any and all sexual orientations (including none) – and that they were not mad nor, as many people think even now, pushing a kink too far.

Lili Elbe was neither the first trans woman to undergo medical treatment, nor was her 'memoir' the first in the field. Karl Baer's story, *Memoirs of a Man's Maiden Years*, was published in 1907, and served as the basis for a 1919 silent movie adaptation. Earl Lind, self-described androgyne, published *Autobiography of an Androgyne* in 1918 and *The Female Impersonators* in 1922. There are several reports, and rumours, of surgical treatment of what we might now call trans men from the 1900s and 1910s. Alan Hart, an American scientist and novelist, underwent his surgical transition in 1917. The first formal, Western medical attempts at 'male-to-female' surgery followed in 1920. 'These early surgical techniques were developing hand in hand with reconstructive and cosmetic surgery methods for war veterans, and in some cases were accompanied by early attempts at hormone therapy. Although there are few detailed accounts within the contemporary medical literature, possibly due to the laws prohibiting castration, there is evidence that multiple surgeries of this nature were performed.' These surgical efforts were well enough known, and considered safe enough that, following Lili Elbe's death, an editorial appeared in community magazine *The World of the Transvestite*. This editorial reaffirmed to its readership the potential of such surgery, noting promising signs coming from Hirschfeld's institute, and included an update from an unnamed transvestite, currently enjoying a postoperative holiday, 'needless to say as a complete woman'.

It isn't just that this erasure of our past is untruthful, although that is a part of it. More, that in nearly every telling of the trans narrative, we are subject to the shock of the new. It's always 'first trans person to': have surgery, publish a book, be employed in profession xyz, serve in the army, have their documents updated, get married in their true gender. It's not about not caring about our milestones, but it is caring about the way in which the need for these firsts overrides the accurate recording of our history. I have heard so many candidates named as 'the first' to have surgery, but even the earliest account I could find, of Herman Karl, is simply the earliest currently known record of modern surgery in a Western context; humans have been modifying their own bodies through self-surgery for thousands of years, and many other cultures have their own accepted forms of modifying the sexed body. Every achievement of the past is cancelled out by the need to label the next achievement 'the first', making the framing of transness the framing of something exotic, different, a symptom of the modern age, rather than as just another aspect of human nature as old as humanity itself. There is no story to sell in that second framing – but there is hope for trans people looking for reassurance of their unremarkableness in an often hostile world.

What would it mean, to trans people now, if our history were common knowledge? By this I do not mean a history of people who are exactly as we are, regardless of the dictates of historical and social context, but of the people whose lives and efforts helped to create the categories, the structures and cultures through which we now move. What if we knew of these figures, these communities, in the same way we know of Oscar Wilde? It's a terrible cliché but, as a young adolescent, I was obsessed with Wilde. I didn't know how to describe my sexuality, and I didn't know how to describe my gender, but I knew that I wanted to be like him. I wanted to be that witty, and that unapologetic – and when the film *Wilde* came out, and I saw that first kiss between two beautiful, passionate men – my body knew that that was what it wanted for itself. Just that little slice of history gave me an insight into myself, and a role model, the comfort of companionship, when I was invisible and alone. What a tremendous gift it would have been, to have known that there were people in that history who might now be called trans, people who lived as the genders they *knew* that they were, regardless of what society had told them. To know that they had claimed their own lives with honesty and courage, and that maybe I could follow their lead and do the same.

The shock of the new doesn't just impact on the telling of our history: it's deeply embedded in the media handling of any trans-related enterprise. So much has been made of the 'groundbreaking' nature of *The Danish Girl*'s approach, and the representation of a trans woman by a cis man has been excused by the reasoning that the film's success would ultimately pave the way for the casting of trans actors. It is, apparently, astonishing to have a mainstream movie with a trans subject matter at all, and the trans community should shelve their objections and be grateful for the increased publicity. As a bit of a movie buff, that explanation didn't sit quite right with me, and it made me curious: is it really so rare for a film to feature the role of a trans woman that Redmayne receiving his Oscar nod is a step forward?

So I decided to watch *The World According to Garp* by way of comparison. I had loved the book when I was younger, but had never got around to seeing the movie. Like *The Danish Girl*, here is a film with a cis man playing a trans woman – like *The Danish Girl*, that man was nominated for an Oscar for his portrayal. This was thirty-four years ago. John Lithgow plays Roberta, an ex-professional football player who now works in the feminist movement and becomes the main character's best friend and anchor of sanity in a mad and often grotesque world. It's not a perfect film, and much of it is firmly of its time. Still, I was struck by how natural Lithgow was in the role, and how firmly Roberta is accepted and celebrated *as a woman* by all the other characters. Not as a man trying to be a woman, not as a particular subset of 'woman' – but just as herself. It was so utterly different from Redmayne's performance, the whole of which seemed to hinge on the open acknowledgement of performance, of gesture, of the sense of being on display. Constantly quivering, seemingly either on the edge of tears or orgasm, wrists held at uncomfortable angles, Redmayne's approximation of what a trans woman is was one of the most uncomfortable things I have been witness to in recent memory. I've always been ambivalent about the casting of cis actors as trans characters, feeling that the more pressing question was the casting of trans actors in all roles. Redmayne changed my mind. The entire edifice felt precisely that – an edifice. Here was transness depicted from the outside, a man disguised through outer trappings, rather than a woman revealed by her own honesty. Shot after shot of stockings, shoes, make-up and wigs, but nothing of the heart of what it is to be trans. It felt almost parodic in its display, and it hurts that that parody will be taken as truth by people who do not know better.

Every project needs a hook. Every artist wants to feel that they have added something new to the cultural landscape. But, in the case of *The Danish Girl*, there is nothing new, simply the recreation, the restaging, of 'the new' by those ignorant of, or unfeeling towards, the history and people they claim to be serving.

Hirschfeld's Institute was pillaged by the Nazis in 1933. One of the most famous images of Nazi book-burning is the documentation of the destruction of his research, his case files, his painstakingly gathered evidence in support of sexual minorities. Hirschfeld died in France in 1935; we do not know exactly how many homosexuals, transvestites and other 'anti-socials' were rounded up and sent to the camps, but we know that the numbers were considerable. Many of those few who survived the war were not freed, but sentenced to further punishment for their 'crimes'. The magazines, bars and organisations that supported the lives of sexual and gendered minorities were gone. The destruction of both Hirschfeld's work and the thriving subcultures that supported and benefited from it set the emerging LGBT rights movement back by decades, if not more so. The drives – legal, social, scientific – towards investigation, knowledge and compassionate acceptance were erased.

We have a chance to relearn that history, and to benefit from and honour that legacy, if we have the will to do so, if we can stand to look at our past without prejudice. I hope that we do.

12

Beyond Binaries

Once you have the desire to see, the tools with which to focus, locate and describe, it is hard to stop finding new ways in which humans do and have done gender.

In the past two years, I have been inundated with media requests to talk about 'non-binary'. Without fail, the journalists and producers asking will refer to the topic as a new trend, something fashionable that can be linked to social media and the latest crop of young celebrities. The reference is always in the singular; 'non-binary' as a noun, not an adjective, like a type of dance or a drug. When we talk, the majority seem disappointed; they don't want to hear about the daily lives, struggles and joys of people of all ages and backgrounds living outside of the binary. The fact that the richness of our experiences cannot be contained in one definition is not the angle they're looking for.

Reactions like these make me realise just how limiting the set-up to our questions of gender beyond binaries is. We assume that anything that is new to us is new to human society as a whole, and that if we don't see it reflected in history textbooks and in recent memory then it cannot have existed for long.

I have always had a love for research, historical research in particular. It was the driving force propelling me into academia, but also a way in which I could locate myself when the world seemed to be spinning out of control

When the rights, and the lives, of people like me are dismissed as irrelevant and modish because of a lack of awareness, a lack of knowledge, history seems ever more important.

It is not that these words – trans, genderqueer, genderfluid, gender-neutral – are timeless categories of human being, appearing in the same way all throughout recorded history. It is that, as far as I and many other researchers can see, there have always been people and categories of people that have troubled and challenged a strict binary of male and female, man and woman.

How are we to fight for what we need now, without learning from what has come before? How can we consider our options, dream bigger and better dreams, ill-equipped and unprepared?

The main argument used against people like me, people who are beyond binaries, is that we cannot, should not, never have existed. Just two examples, initially found by accident during my musicological research, begin to show that ideas of a third or 'other' gender are not merely a modern invention.

Despite the importance of the Byzantine Empire in the development of European culture – particularly in matters of religion – it is not given much of a look-in in most British schools. I learnt about the Greeks, the Romans and the Egyptians, but it was only when I became serious about music history and early music that I encountered the long history of Byzantium. Of immediate interest was the prevalence and importance of eunuchs in Byzantine rule and general society. To many of us, the word 'eunuch' conjures up an orientalist fantasy image of a lisping, scheming creature guarding a harem; the truth is so much wider and more interesting than that stereotype allows. Up to the ninth century, 'eunuch' could mean many things: a sterile man, an impotent man, celibate men and women who abstained from sex for religious reasons, men who castrated themselves to better follow intellectual pursuits, men who castrated themselves as a form of birth control, men who castrated themselves to gain a position reserved for eunuchs, men who were castrated as children by their families for career reasons, and illegitimate male children of the royal line castrated to preserve the purity of the ruling lineage. Throughout the Byzantine Empire, eunuchs existed in a gender category other than that of men or women, and were found in all kinds of roles. Eunuchs were generals, soldiers, political advisers, bishops, members of the royal court, musicians, entertainers, secretaries, monks, priests, barbers and doctors. Some believed that eunuchs found it unnaturally easy to be chaste, others that all eunuchs were unnaturally lascivious. Eunuchs were seen as fundamentally virtuous, and also fundamentally prone to moral weaknesses; the category contained multitudes. For around a thousand years, the 'other' gender category of the eunuch waxed and waned throughout the many countries of the Byzantine Empire: the persistence and strength of such a category cannot be dismissed as a fluke or a curiosity.

It was partly through the example of the Byzantine

eunuchs that our second example was formed. For all that I had read about gendered history, and general music history, before beginning my undergraduate music degree, I had no concept of the castrati. When our history of opera lecturer first mentioned them, I couldn't believe that such a fundamental part of musical development and musical history could be so easily hidden away. My attention was captured and, after retraining as a singer, I found that the music written for these voices suited mine. A popular revival of early operatic music, particularly that of Handel, has seen an awareness of the castrati grow but still the embarrassment and confusion over this category remains.

Castrati is the plural for the castrated singers whose talents lie at the heart of the development of Western opera. Operated upon just before, or around, the emergence of puberty, the aim of castration was to preserve a high voice in a (modified) male body, finely crafted through some of the most rigorous musical training the world has ever seen. Some boys volunteered for the procedure; the majority did not. The changes wrought by castration were not limited to the voice, but created a range of body types that blurred the limits of male and female. The Church, so usually opposed to sexual deviation, was instrumental in the rise and popularity of the castrati. Due to papal rules, no woman could perform on the stages of Rome; castrati played the female parts. Throughout the rest of Europe, but most particularly in Italy and London, castrati were the heroes of the opera stage: the gods, kings and lovers of the seventeenth, eighteenth and even early nineteenth centuries. Mocked by some, their beauty and talents were celebrated by others: the best castrati singers were the toast of high society and the confidants of kings. Casanova, in his memoirs, remarked that the erotic effect of the castrati was so strong it forced every man to become a pederast, and having a castrato lover was a mark of success for an aristocratic lady. The libretti of the time made no bones about the confusion of categories the castrati inspired – *La finta pazza* (1641) gives these lines to our cross-dressed, castrato hero:

> *Sweet change of nature,*
> *A woman transforming herself into a man,*
> *A man transforming himself into a woman …*
> *How many of you envy my state,*
> *That of being both a man and a girl?*

To add to the gendered free-for-all, the roles created for castrati singers could also be sung by women *en travesti*. There were rumours that some of the best female singers were secretly castrati, and vice versa. To paraphrase much of the research into early operatic staging: the confusion as to which body could be found under the costume added to the erotic and dramatic thrill.

Castrati singers were the scandalous sex symbols of the operatic stage, and also the pure conduits for the religious music of the Sistine Chapel. The last remaining castrato singer, Alessandro Moreschi, died in 1922. Their presence was not limited to the musical fringes, but is wound in and out of Enlightenment culture, European society, our broader artistic and social roots.

It is an appalling wrong that so many children were abused in this way: there can be no dispute there. But I cannot help but ask what this says about our society, just two hundred, three hundred years ago – that we seemed to have such a need for an 'other' that we created one with knives, with music, with costumes – and then, in deference to emerging nineteenth-century ideas about sex, about gender – tried to write it out of the musical canon. Musicological writers in the late nineteenth and early twentieth centuries treat the castrati phenomenon as a collective embarrassment, something not to be spoken of, to be forgotten if possible. And yet here they are – in our opera houses, our palaces, our art galleries, our libraries – a man-made third gender category that, once, was celebrated the continent over.

Of course, it was not just in high society that gender variance was found. While researching the castrati, and the *en travesti* women who sang alongside them, I had my eyes opened to the wealth of historical examples of gender beyond the binary that existed off the stage during the same time period. Wealth, scandal, fame and social influence provided protection to the castrati. Not so to the ordinary people of the same eras who defied the limits of what was meant by man or woman.

Glossed in some histories as proto-gay men, the majority of researchers now consider the molly a third gender category of their own. A feminine 'sodomite', the molly was often considered quite different from the other men who desired men and who congregated in taverns, private houses, alleyways and parks in the hope of sex and, possibly, love and community. Historian Theo van der Meer, in his analysis of Early Modern same-sex practices, describes numerous ways in which mollies were differentiated from masculine men who desired men: through hair removal, speech patterns, styles of dress and differences in body weight and femininity of movement. A police report from Paris in 1748 describes a group of mollies thus: '[They] put handkerchiefs on their heads, imitating women, mincing like them. When there was some new young man there, they called him the Bride, and in this case, he comes the object of everybody.' In other contemporaneous reports, these mollies are distinguished by their softness and their swaying hips. In the privacy of their own clubs, they carried out rituals of marriage and mock childbirth.

Alongside the category of 'molly' there was the 'tom': an additional gendered label that was not quite female and not quite male. Not just a passing woman (a woman living as a man) and not only a woman who desired other women – both of these categories existed in their own right, and same-sex desire did not require masculine habits – the tom blended masculine and feminine gendered fashions, mannerisms and characteristics to signify something other.

These were not the only ways in which the binary was broken. We know of the drag balls of the nineteenth century, and the Neapolitan tradition of *femminiello*, a term which cannot be parsed as either 'gay man' or 'trans woman', and which continues to this day. In diaries, letters, pamphlets and pornography, we find rich and varied evidence for the fact that Early Modern and Modern European culture is suffused with gendered expressions that cannot be conveyed by either 'man' or 'woman' alone.

Sadly, though, some of our clearest evidence comes from the records of the courts, extending from the Middle Ages until the end of the eighteenth century. The threat of punishment, ever present, frequently translated into reality for those without money or status to protect them. Four examples from across these years show how dangerous it could be to challenge the gender binary.

Victims were usually charged under laws concerning sodomy, but it is clear that sodomy was not the main crime on trial. After all, the historical record is full of instances of same-sex sex, same-sex desire, and sodomy between people of all sexes. What is apparent in cases that came to trial is the ways in which the gendered transgressions of the accused are seen to be beyond the law. Bernd-Ulrich Hergemöller explains the case of Rolandino Ronchaia, burnt to death in Venice in 1354:

> Since childhood he had never felt any 'natural desire' for a woman. He had left the woman he had married in Padua and had settled in Venice. Since he had the voice, face, demeanour and breasts of a woman, people had regarded him only as a woman and had called him 'Rolandina'. He had given men exactly the same pleasure as women gave them.

In London, in 1395, a similar case was tried, with a similar outcome. John/Eleanor Rykener presented as both a man and a woman, depending on circumstances, and made their living through sex work. They were arrested, and burnt at the stake.

Some passing women, in reality and in songs and stories, were lauded for their courage in living as men. Whether they were celebrated or condemned usually came down to three factors: whether they insisted on maintaining their male gender, whether they had had sex as a man, and whether they had modified their bodies in ways which threatened to usurp the 'naturalness' of the sex binary. Many reasons have been given as to why people assigned as female would spend their lives as men: for romance, for practical reasons, for adventure. There is, of course, another possibility: that these people were men, self-declared, or were some other gender known only to themselves. What is clear is that the compulsion to live freely was greater than the compulsion to live in safety. In 1477, in Germany, Katherina Hetzeldorfer was tried for living as a man and using a phallus; this phallus was strapped on, used for sex and could be urinated through. Hetzeldorfer was found guilty, and drowned. Even more scandalous was the case of Catherina Linck in 1721. The key point of Linck's prosecution was not just that they lived as a man, marrying one woman and having sex with many others, but that they used their leather phallus (complete with scrotum) for both vaginal penetration and for oral sex. The combined crimes of gender usurpation and sodomy were too much to be borne. Linck was executed by beheading.

There are so many lessons we could learn from these examples, from the thousands more we find when we widen our historical scope. But this is the most important: that a strict gender binary has never been able to hold the totality of humanity – not in the past, not in the present – not in the future.

But what now? If we are not just a flash in the pan, and cannot be forced back into binary bounds, then what are we left with and where do we go? What are the ramifications of this knowledge, not just for those of us outside of the binary, but for everyone?

The most basic must come first: recognition and protection

under the law. It shocks many people to learn that some-one like me occupies a legal grey area, and that my right to employment, to public services, to live free from harass-ment, is arguably not covered by law. I say arguably because whether or not I'm protected by Equalities Law is a question I can't get a straight answer to. The lawyers I've spoken to have said 'no'. The civil servants I've spoken to have said 'yes'. From the number of people who've denied me services, failed to pay me for transphobic reasons, insulted me in job interviews because of my gender, refused to take attacks on me and people like me seriously, I think it's safe to say that – practically speaking – we are not protected. It seems clear that, in order to gain these protections, we need to con-vince those making the law that we are a recognisable group entitled to specific inclusion in human rights and equalities legislation.

Only a handful of countries worldwide recognise anything other than a gender binary, and those that do recognise something other than male or female do not always protect the rights of those so categorised. Nepal, Thailand, New Zealand, Australia, Pakistan and Bangladesh offer some limited recognition of a third gender category, with New Zealand leading the way. The movement, globally, is grow-ing, but the resistance to change is profound.

The UK government is under constant petition to recognise the rights of those outside the binary, but the response so far has been discouraging. A 2015 petition pushing for full legal equality for all trans people was officially dismissed. On the subject of people outside the gender binary, the Ministry of Justice had this to say: 'The Equality Act 2010 protects people from discrimination if it arises from their being perceived as either male or female. We recognise that a very small number of people consider themselves to be of neither gender. We are not aware that that results in any specific detriment.' Dismayed, my activist colleagues and I decided to collect some facts on the specific detriment suffered, and present these findings to the Ministry of Justice. Of those who responded to our call for information, 94 per cent reported feeling unsafe because of their gender expression. Respondents told us of the lack of provisions in education, work, housing and health care, and said that they faced a daily choice between being misgendered and being denied access. There were widespread experiences of being bullied at school and abused at work, being labelled 'difficult', 'dangerous' and 'unprofessional'. Some respondents told us of the sexual abuse they'd suffered because of their gender, and others of their doctors' refusal to treat them. The data we collected was strikingly similar to other research into trans lives, but with the specific problem of being recognisable enough to be abused, but not recognisable enough to be counted and protected.

Our meeting with the Ministry of Justice to discuss their response and these findings was pleasant enough, but evidently failed to change their minds. The results of the first parliamentary backed, nationwide survey into trans experiences, the cross-party Trans Inquiry, were published at the beginning of 2016. The inquiry supported the need for non-binary recognition and protection; the government response, six months later, dismissed it. Barack Obama, challenged on trans issues by non-binary activist Maria Munir, gave a more positive and supportive response to our concerns than I have heard expressed by any UK civil servant or government official. Trans people who are not men or women are just as subject to transphobic discrimination and oppression as trans men and women – but we continue to be dismissed as a tiny and unimportant group of fantasists.

Many such people, then, would prefer to put their efforts into effecting broader cultural changes. We may be reduced to a trend, but at least it's a foot in the door. The societal shifts we're now seeing, as much as I want and need more, are greater than I ever thought possible when I first came out. When I was a teenager, anything other than a strict adherence to gendered stereotypes in appearance was an invitation to bullying. Teenagers now can look to fellow teenager, Hollywood royalty Jaden Smith, modelling womenswear for Louis Vuitton and refuses to limit himself with traditional male/female stereotypes and behaviours. Genderfluid celebrity Ruby Rose has become infamous for a desirability that transcends labels, and Miley Cyrus has been open about her experiences of identifying as multiple genders. What we're seeing in pop culture is a reflection of the opening up of gendered categories and behaviours happening in everyday life. Research by Daphna Joel of Tel Aviv University, in 2013, found that feelings of being, to a greater or lesser extent, 'the other gender', 'both genders' and/or 'neither gender' are far more common than previously supposed: over a third of respondents to the study reported such feelings. A recent YouGov poll found that around 20 per cent of people placed themselves on a spectrum between male and female. Millennials are far more likely to see themselves as between, both, neither, or other, than older age groups, and this development shows no signs of stopping.

It certainly tallies with my own experiences. Being obviously, openly, neither/nor seems to have made me something of a confessional box. I realise that this is a self-selecting sample, but believe there is still truth here. For half my life, people who are not trans, or not openly trans, who would still answer to 'woman' or 'man', have been telling me that they don't really feel themselves to be at peace with those categories. The reasons are many, and mostly to do with the crushing pressure of stereotypes and expected behaviours. What is universal is the reporting of the fact that what they are told they *are*, from the outside in, doesn't chime with who they feel themselves to be beneath the exterior. Their feelings about gender are more confused, more questioning and less stable than their outer behaviour would have an observer believe. I wonder how common these feelings are. I wonder what further research, and further exposure to openly gender non-conforming people, will show us.

Our steps towards equality are still tentative – this is not a done deal. For every example of positive change I could provide, I could show multiple negatives. But the changes I have seen, over my lifetime, at least show that change is possible. What I have learnt about our histories shows me that the gendered bars and limits placed around us need not be permanent.

Above all, over and over again, I am shown the many and varied ways in which the gender binary simply does not exist.

All I can hope is to live long enough to see that that knowledge take root, and blossom.

13

The T from the LGB

Faced with a blurring, shifting, evolving landscape of what gender and identity can mean, many people would like to try to make things appear simpler. For some cis LGB people, and some straight trans people, this means marking a neat line dividing issues around gender identity from issues around sexual orientation. Gender is who you are, and sexuality is who you want; sexual orientation is who you go to bed *with* and gender identity is who you go to bed *as*. To avoid confusion, to avoid misgendering, it would be easier to part ways; get rid of the alphabet soup of LGBT(+Q)(+I)(+A) and focus solely on trans issues, or solely on LGB issues.

Some of the reasons for this desire are valid if not, perhaps, readily discernible to an outsider. After all, one of the reasons why we're so often seen as the same group is one of the reasons why some of us want to go our separate ways. In the public imagination, and in the particular reasoning of people who either don't know or don't like trans people, being trans is what happens when you take being gay too far. This line of argument has two strands. The first, popular with those who mock gay and trans people alike, is that gay men are girly and gay women are butch: what is a trans woman but a really girly man, a trans man but a super-butch woman? The second explanation is more often trotted out by cis gay men and lesbians who disapprove of trans people. They believe that every trans person is actually a gay person so scared of being gay that they would physically alter their bodies so as to make their desires seem more normal. It is unsurprising that many trans people, sick of being called fantasists or cowards, would prefer to strike out on their own. It's also unsurprising that cis gay people, sick of being told that they 'want to be a man' or 'want to be a woman', actually want to make it clear that being gender non-conforming and queer is not the same thing, or not always the same thing, as being trans.

There's also the issue of transphobia in LGBT spaces. For all the joint statements from campaigning groups and advocates, and the ways in which we are lumped together by outsiders, there's a sizeable chunk of the LGB population that hates trans people just as much as straight people do. We feel it in the ways we are groped on the dance floor of a gay club by someone who wants to 'check', and in the refusal to allow queer trans people access to queer spaces, because we're not seen as legitimate. It's in the treatment of our trans bodies in these spaces and communities, the ways in which they are described as disgusting, freakish, threatening and just plain wrong. The cis gay men who claim that vaginas are gross, little thinking that there are gay men with vaginas. Cis lesbians who describe their lesbianism not as a love of women, but as a rejection of penis, and woe betide the lesbian who might have one, or might have had one once. It was, until recently, the way that mainstream LGBT organisations were happy to tack a 'T' on the end, but not to fight for trans rights, inclusion, justice. There is so much bad blood, and so much still to fix.

My stake in all of this is personal. As a queer trans person, it has to be. But beyond my own needs there are wider, far more compelling reasons, why trying to pull the T from out of the LGB hurts more than it heals. In our interlockings, our intersections, there is power, hope, a path to something better. But the divisions that would drag us back have existed for a long time, and cannot be wished away. We have to go deeper if we wish to go forward.

In the public imagination, most trans people are assumed to be straight. After all, this is one of the main props of the standard trans story: 'I knew I was a woman, because I needed to be with a man *as* a woman', and vice versa. It may be surprising, then, to learn that trans people are far more likely to be bisexual, gay or lesbian than cis people are.

Anecdotally, we know this and have known this for a long time. In my own UK trans community the number of straight trans people I know is overwhelmed by the bi, queer, pansexual, omnisexual, lesbian and gay trans people of all genders and descriptors. Some of these trans people are heavily invested in the mainstream gay scene, and many have made alternative, trans-friendly spaces where they can express honestly, and without fear of reprisal, both their desires and their selfhoods. Our trans community is also comprised of people with no sexual desire towards others, who may or may not be in romantic relationships that are gay or queer. Some of us are in open relationships, some of us are in polyamorous triads, some are happy to be single, some are monogamously coupled. We are into kink, into vanilla sex, into no sex at all, and some trans people combine these categories in ways we have not been taught to recognise or respect. It is not that straight trans people don't exist, because of course they do. But I don't know where, in this proposed splitting of LGB from T, we would fit the majority of trans people who are both.

Research data backs up the evidence of our lives. There are patterns and changes that shift depending on culture, location, subsets of identity, but the broad findings leave little doubt as to the importance of LGBQ desires in many trans people's lives. A 2013 Canadian study found that an estimated 63.3 per cent of trans men were bisexual, gay, queer, or otherwise found themselves attracted to other men. The authors of this work referred back to similar studies from other researchers, in 2001 and 2011, which found that between one quarter and one half of trans men describe themselves as gay or bisexual, with even more preferring the broader term 'queer'. Likewise, there have been numerous reports that have demonstrated the fact that around the same numbers of trans women would also describe themselves as lesbian, bisexual and/or queer. Scottish Transgender Alliance's enormously important 2012 report on trans mental health found that the majority of trans people surveyed described themselves as bisexual (27 per cent) or queer (24 per cent). Many respondents used multiple terms to convey the nuances of their sexual orientation.

There are trans people whose orientations remain fixed throughout transition, and there are also people who find that their sexuality can shift and change throughout life.

Some attribute this to hormonal changes, others to the ways in which being trans forced them to question many of the received truths they'd previously accepted, making them more open to possibilities previously seen as impossible. I know of many trans masculine people who were not attracted to men pre-transition, but who found themselves identifying as bisexual or gay post-transition. Many said that they couldn't imagine relating to a man in a perceived heterosexual relationship, but that being with a man as a visible man made sense.

For myself, being genderqueer and being queer are intimately linked, calling back to the same need to resist limits on who I might be and who I might desire. I don't want to second-guess the direction of my life from past experiences, while still needing words to describe the particularities of those experiences to others. I know many trans people who feel the same way about their sexualities, whatever those sexualities might be: that there is no point where you could extract one from the other, could draw a clean line through the totality of a person. I get very tired of the idea that LGB rights means only LGB *cis* rights. I can't countenance the exclusion of trans queer people with the idea that trans here is a noun, something separate, rather than an adjective that points to a broad range of experiences, placing us in community with queer people of all genders.

These intersections between gender and sexuality are not simply products of our modern lives, but vital components of the groups and movements that have made our lives possible. Not that we could guess that from the majority of gay and lesbian histories – *Surpassing the Love of Men, Gay Life and Culture*: *A World History*, *Who's Who in Gay and Lesbian History* – but the actual record of same-sex desire in human cultures is threaded through with evidence of gender non-conforming lives. Previous cis historians have tried to gloss that variance as 'gay'. More recent researchers have stressed the importance of taking everyone – even those in the past – on their own terms. And those terms are often more mixed and complicated than our modern categories of 'cis' and 'trans', 'gay' and 'straight'.

The very word 'homosexual', used so exclusively now, initially had a double meaning, being both the desire for the same sex, and possessing a mind, a brain, belonging to the 'opposite sex'. 'Homosexual' was neither trans nor gay, but a root from which both of these modern ideas grew. Karl Ulrichs, one of the early founders of what would become the later LGBT movement, defined homosexuality as a third sex; the people so often described as gay men in modern tellings of this story were described by Ulrichs as having, as he did, 'a woman's soul trapped in the wrong body'. There is a tendency now, stemming from the gay liberation movement of the 1970s, to call those explanations excuses, a way of trying to garner sympathy, or explain the unexplainable. In societies that punished same-sex behaviour, surely it made sense to claim a kind of heterosexuality? But the fact is, when we delve deeply, we find all kinds of genders, gendered explanations, in these early movements and communities, and many people who experienced same-sex desires without any hint of gender variance.

A clear comparison can be found in the early twentieth-century examples of Radclyffe/John Hall and Natalie Barney. Both are most commonly described as lesbians: they lived at the same time, had many friends in common, moved in similar queer circles. And yet their approaches to gender and desire were totally different. Hall is most famous for her/his groundbreaking 1928 novel *The Well of Loneliness*, which was banned in Britain under obscenity laws. The tragic story of congenital invert Stephen Gordon, *The Well* is known both as the quintessential early lesbian text and also as one of the most depressing and, to many lesbian readers, unconvincing stories of same-sex desire in the canon. Vita Sackville-West, Violet Trefusis and Virginia Woolf all found it wanting. Hall's depiction of physically, mentally masculine inverts, doomed by their treacherous bodies to an outcast life could not be more removed from the kind of lesbianism celebrated by Natalie Barney, depicted in *The Well* as Stephen's friend Valérie Seymour. Barney, an American heiress and founder of one of the most famous salons in Paris, believed in the innate superiority of women in all things, and in the passionate, erotic celebration of femininity. She was unabashedly open about her love for other women, believing lesbianism to be a more moral, and certainly more rewarding, choice than heterosexuality. When it comes to Hall, I don't even know which name or pronoun to use. Hall was John and he to those who knew him well and respected his inner life, and Radclyffe and she to the rest of the world. None of us could know whether, if he/she lived now, they would be a trans man, a butch lesbian or something else entirely. What we do know is that our shared past often defies current categories in favour of something more murky and complex. We can see a recognition of that complexity in the ways in which some early homosexual campaigners tried to reject it: something must exist in order for it to be suppressed. The 'movement for masculine culture' was set up in opposition to the more popular theories of inversion and gender/sexual variance, positioning homosexuality as something manly, virile and utterly unconnected to the cross-dressing and cross-gendered behaviours of the abnormal. Biologist Benedict Friedländer, a misogynist, anti-Semitic Jewish man, was one of the leaders of this movement, in which nationalism, machismo, sexism and racism combined with notions of a biological drive towards homosexuality to demonstrate the supposed superiority of the white, same-sex-oriented man.

As we have already seen, sodomy laws were enforced with greater regularity, and with greater cruelty, upon the people who broke the gendered rules of their societies. Early Modern European culture is so rich with depictions of same-sex sex and desire, but it is in the records of arrests, torture and executions that we find much of our evidence of gender non-conforming behaviours. The ways in which we have interpreted this evidence change, of course, with the meaning we wish to find. The figure of the passing woman appears over and over again in lesbian history and historical fiction as an example of the lengths women will go to when denied the chance to love other women openly. Increasingly, I'm finding the same stories passed around trans circles as evidence that trans people have always existed. We all of us want to feel validated, to feel the legitimising force of history – but do we ever have the right to claim strangers as being one of our own?

We certainly feel the draw. Louis Sullivan, himself a pioneer in the record of trans history, wrote a biography of Californian man Jack Garland, who died in 1936. Jack could be seen as a typical example of the passing woman: assigned female at birth, an adventurer in men's clothes, 'the mysterious girl-boy, man-woman, or what-is-it' in the newspaper parlance of the day. He was a soldier, a nurse, and, eventually, just another man like any other, until the shock of his autopsy. But then there is the fact that Jack acknowledged his need to be with men as a man, that he made many coded references to life on the street with hobos and 'willy boys'. His closest friend had no doubt that he was a man through and through, despite his birth. Others, after his death, have crafted stories of him as a woman pushed to imitation by the constraints of misogyny. Louis Sullivan described him, without a doubt, as a trans man. How could any of us place him, in a way that does him justice, when we can never ask and know for sure?

Even when divisions between categories of gender and sexuality came into force, shared oppressions meant a shared battle. The American protests and riots of the early sixties – Dewey's, Compton's – were melting pots of different identities. Even the most famous riot of them all, the one that many people cite as *the* birthplace of the modern LGBT movement, was not a single-community affair. Contrary to the story presented in Roland Emmerich's *Stonewall*, the Stonewall riots were the bubbling up of all the injustices borne by gender non-conforming people – trans women of colour, butch black lesbians, transvestites, femmes, sex workers, queens – the queer people who suffered the most from police violence and societal rejection. Stormé DeLarverie, Marsha P. Johnson, Miss Major, Sylvia Rivera: we owe so much to them, and the countless others who were brave enough to say 'enough is enough'. Without their actions at Stonewall, the modern gay movement, the rights enjoyed by gay people, would be unthinkable. And yet, even then, there were cis gay people, white people, trying to exclude the trans and/or gender non-conforming activists from the movement that they themselves had made. The Gay Liberation Front, co-founded by trans people, moved to exclude their own founders. Sylvia Rivera and Marsha P. Johnson started STAR – Street Transvestite Action Revolutionaries – a group that helped trans street kids survive, gave them shelter, food, education, hope. They did it without the help of the new gay groups. After their exclusion from the GLF, some trans, gender non-conforming people started the QLF – the Queens' Liberation Front – only to find themselves banned from the first ever march to commemorate Stonewall. There are harsh truths for cis gay people to be found in the *TransLiberation Newsletter* of 1971:

The oppression against transvestites and transsexuals of either sex arises from sexist values and this oppression is manifested by homosexuals and heterosexuals alike in the form of exploitation, ridicule, harassment, beating, rapes, murders and the use of us as shock troops and sacrificial victims.

Trans lesbians led the way in many second-wave feminist groups, only to find themselves excluded from lesbian feminist spaces. Clubs, communities, activist organisations where trans queer people created and defined what it meant to be LGBT, fought for justice, did the constant, dulling, dangerous work of being out and demanding more: those same organisations turned their backs on their trans members once it was safe to do so. Some of our modern history is extraordinary in what it shows us of cooperation and compassion, and some of it is a masterclass in excluding the most marginalised 'for the greater good' of the most privileged.

I don't think this mixed bag of our history is a sign that we should try to part ways; that tactic, too, is scattered throughout the historical record, and it hasn't worked yet. Instead, as ever, we have a chance to learn from the mistakes of the past, to examine those exclusions, these moments of cowardice and hubris, and to apply what we have learnt to our current movements and communities. We could take the best – the empathy and solidarity – and try to add to it, to pass that legacy down to the people who come after us. Not just as activists, but as individuals, we can do better in community than in division.

Many people, confronted with a picture of transgender pioneer Leslie Feinberg, on being told that she was transgender (without the use of that pronoun), would assume that this meant that Feinberg was a trans man. They would think that his sexuality would be based on a foundation of maleness; gay to mean attracted to men, straight to mean attracted to women. Those assumptions would be wrong. Feinberg, whose fiction and non-fiction books changed the lives of so many trans people, myself included, was a transgender, butch lesbian. She used different pronouns in different spaces, insisted on the importance of solidarity, and linked her trans activism to her communism, her anti-racist work, her support for trade unions and her feminism. In a 2006 interview, she explained the importance of having the right word in the right context when it came to expressing the self:

For me, pronouns are always placed within context. I am female-bodied, I am a butch lesbian, a transgender lesbian – referring to me as 'she/her' is appropriate, particularly in a non-trans setting in which referring to me as 'he' would appear to resolve the social contradiction between my birth sex and gender expression and render my transgender expression invisible. I like the gender neutral pronoun 'ze/hir' because it makes it impossible to hold on to gender/sex/sexuality assumptions about a person you're about to meet or you've just met. And in an all trans setting, referring to me as 'he/him' honors my gender expression in the same way that referring to my sister drag queens as 'she/her' does.

Constantly, in Feinberg's work, there is the referring back to multiples: multiple communities, multiple experiences, multiple ways of naming and being named. She died in 2014 at the age of sixty-five. She was survived by her partner of many years, Minnie Bruce Pratt, another writer whose works reverberate with the knowledge of what it is to trouble the boundaries of how we are supposed to express our genders and desires. Pratt writes of being femme, of locating femme in the radical repositioning of the world's gendered power norms, provoking investigation into what it learnt, what is 'natural' and what feels right. Her words challenge the reader to re-evaluate what it is that they know about bodies, categories and love, and dares them to see something more than they previously thought possible. Her description of making love with a partner, presumably Feinberg, who has strapped on a phallus, in her 1995 collection *S/He*, asks us how we can define the limits of other people's lives:

You are a woman who has been accused of betraying womanhood. In my groans of pleasure from your cock, perhaps some would say I have betrayed womanhood with you, that we are traitors to our sex. You refusing to allow the gestures of what is called masculinity to be preempted by men. Me refusing to relinquish the ecstasies of surrender to women who can only call it subservience. Traitors to our sex, or spies and explorers across the boundaries of what is man, what is woman?

How can you pull apart a life like Feinberg's, like Pratt's? Why would anyone want to do so?

Part of being trans, of being queer – not all of it, not for all people, but part – is in the reimagining of what it is to be human. These are categories forged from the failure or refusal to acquiesce to majority rule. That majority rule requires nice, clear lines and limits, and so often we, who are fighting for acceptance, will try to stick to the same in imitation. Too often, all we do in doing so is hurt our own. I'm not prepared to accept any definition of trans, any definition of LGB, that would leave out those like Feinberg and Pratt. I think we would all be the sorrier for it.

If we have any hope of trying to end the ignorance, discrimination and violence that blight our lives, we cannot afford to be seduced by the sophistry of single-issue movements. As Audre Lorde so rightly said, we do not live single-issue lives. The idea of single-issue movements, of whatever kind, so often has the idea of 'neutrality' at its heart; an LGB cause where LGB means cis and white, a trans movement where trans means straight and white. But none of us is 'neutral';

some of us just have less pressure, less hatred to contend with than others. Focusing on the needs of those with a lighter burden to bear is not 'objective' or 'pragmatic', but it is a confirmation of historic societal prejudices that say that some lives matter more than others, some lives are too 'complicated' to be worth caring for, some oppressions are just too entrenched to change.

We talk of an LGBT umbrella, but not of those LGBT people who cannot seek shelter beneath because we have narrowed our protections down to the point that only the few are covered. We have been taught to weigh up lives and accord them value, and we turn that tactic on each other. When we feel anger, we direct it towards the most vulnerable members of our communities for their failure to be 'respectable' enough to toe the party line, to make themselves acceptable to those who hate us.

I want, and I need, an LGBT umbrella, but what I need beyond that is a solution to the injustice raining down on us – and my needs are less pressing, less desperate, than many others'.

So I am wary of any call to split the T from the LGB, rather than to focus on specific needs within broader community with shared resources, shared strength. It feels too close to washing our hands of those who stand in the way of assimilation, who would demand justice instead of tolerance – who cannot cut themselves into pieces to fit a truncated agenda.

14

Trans Feminisms

Despite my fear of cameras, I'm slowly getting used to being filmed, under certain circumstances: live performances, music videos, documentaries and educational projects. I'm still a novice when it comes to television. Earlier this year I was asked to appear on a flagship UK news programme, a live broadcast, to discuss proposed changes to the way the law recognises and treats trans people. In that total slowing down of time that happens during a performance, it was impossible not to read the host's teleprompter just before she introduced me and her other guest; I was labelled there as a 'trans activist', and the writer picked for her opposing views was 'a feminist'. It was so hard not to interrupt, mostly to laugh, and ask why it was that she was a feminist and I was not? My doctoral research is in feminist musicology; I specifically applied to my university because of its groundbreaking work in music and gender. A feminist attitude underscores all of my musical performances and event organising, my teaching and my charity work. I made my first feminist speech when I was ten years old, and I began writing for online and offline feminist publications in my mid-teens. It would have been just as easy to say 'trans feminist' as 'trans activist' – and yet that word, that label that makes sense of my life, was not given me.

I need feminism. I need it not because I am a woman but because, no matter what lens the world uses to view me through, I am subject to gender-based abuses, founded on the idea that there is one, hierarchical, coercive gender system. When I am seen as a gender non-conforming woman, a failed woman, a dyke and a bitch, I need feminism. When I am seen as a gender non-conforming man, a pretty boy, a poof, a faggot, I need feminism. Most of all, when I am seen as the flipped version of what I am – a gender failure and a gendered freak – then I need a way of fighting back, of changing the world that treats me this way. Feminism is my method of resistance, my roadmap to change.

This enforcing of gendered systems, of gendered expectations – the poor treatment that comes from being seen as 'not right' and 'not important' in the scheme of gender – can come from all places and all people. The first man who groped me in broad daylight as a young teenager, a straight man, and the man in a packed nightclub who forced his face between my legs, who kept coming back to grab my genitals, because 'It's okay, I'm gay'. The woman who took advantage of my age and my vulnerability, and seeing me naked and alone after a shower in a public changing room, put her arm around me and asked me to take my towel off and get dressed in front of her, and the drunk woman after Pride who asked me if I was a man or a woman, then answered her own question with a blow to my crotch. I have been extremely lucky, compared with many women, compared with many people outside of the binary, compared, in fact, to many men who have also suffered from the effects of misogyny. But I don't believe that any of these experiences are acceptable. It's not that I want a weapon with which to attack the individuals behind these instances, but that I need a total game plan that ensures that these instances, any instance of gendered violence, any system of gendered oppression, becomes a thing of the past.

It's hardly as though I'm alone here: all of my friends, and the majority of my trans community, are feminists. They are engaged with feminist communities that reflect the kind of belief expressed by South African activist and artist Gabrielle Le Roux, describing here her awakening to the importance of trans people in feminist practice:

> Through a couple of close personal friendships, I began to deeply engage with transgender issues as gender issues and realised that this is all our issue ... This means that a struggle for gender equality founded on the idea that we are struggling for equity between men and women is also profoundly flawed. Having worked as a feminist activist for two decades with so many issues and such diverse women, for us not to have engaged with transgender issues as gender issues made me feel cheated. Gender is the connection between transgender and feminism – I feel strongly that until we engage with transgender and inter-sex inclusively as gender issues, our feminisms are stuck.

And yet, we have headlines like these:

'Call yourself a woman? Feminists take on transgender community in bitter debate'

'What Is a Woman? The dispute between radical feminism and transgenderism'

'The Conflict Between Feminism And The Transgender Movement'

'Transgender Rights Versus Feminism: What makes a woman?'

They crop up in right- and left-wing publications alike; it's the standard set-up for news discussion shows. Many trans people I know have given up on mainstream media engagement, the kind of talking-head appearances from experts, because of the inevitability of being pitted against a transphobic feminist, and of being encouraged to fight.

This framing refuses to jibe with what I know to be true about the multiplicity of feminisms in general, and the history and import of trans feminism in particular.

Trans women have been part of feminist movements for a long time. When we look at the magazines of the queer, radical German subcultures of the 1920s and 1930s we see trans and lesbian writers and communities sharing spaces, publications, clubs and activist groups. Many trans men, like influential philanthropist Reed Erickson, had been feminists (and sometimes lesbians) before transitioning, and retained strong ties to feminist movements. Pioneers of all genders from the older, working-class bar and drag scenes – black, Latin and white – were fighting for gendered freedom and justice long before the theoretical developments of 1960s and 1970s second-wave feminism. And yet it was a minority of these second-wavers that created and legitimised the idea that 'real' feminism could not include or even support trans people – and which singled out trans women for a vicious campaign of abuse.

There are three arguments lobbied again and again at trans people, supposedly from a feminist perspective, supposedly from a neutral, unbiased position. From a distance, without repetition and investigation, these arguments can look reasonable. But the uncritical assumption that these arguments are correct may well, in the long run, be causing more harm to trans people than the more open abuse of a furious minority.

The first is that trans people, by existing, by transitioning, prop up a sexist gender binary. This argument relies, as a point of principle, on the erasure of trans people like me, who do not fit into a gender binary and have no wish to do so. Further 'evidence' is provided by images of some trans men and women in the mainstream media: glamorous, feminine women and masculine, blokey men. What is missing here, apart from an awareness of the diversity of gender expressions and identities to be found across trans communities, is knowledge of the ways in which medical treatment for trans people has been granted or denied based on the expectations of cis, mainly male, clinicians. Pioneering sexologist Harry Benjamin was famous for his criteria of what made a 'true transsexual', but sexual stereotyping in the provision of trans-related care is still with us. Trans people have been denied hormones and surgery for being gay, for being bisexual, for being too tall or too short, too fat or too thin, for not moulding themselves into white Western presentations of gender, for daring to be butch trans women, or femme trans men, for being disabled, for giving the 'wrong' answers to intrusive questions about sex and masturbation, for not being in full-time employment, for being married, for refusing to change their names and for being intersex. Those examples come from the lives of trans people I have met, have known, in real life, and I suspect that there are many more. Some trans people have to play the long game: give cis clinicians what they're looking for so as to be able to transition, and then have the space, the freedom, to present as is right. If the feminists who used this argument truly cared about coercive gender standards they would be standing *with* trans people and demanding the end to medical gatekeeping – and, yet, here we are. The behaviour of those with power over us is used as a stick with which to beat us. It solves nothing.

The second common feminist argument made against trans people is that gender may be diverse, but sex is binary, unchanging and oppositional. We have already seen some of the ways in which sex and gender are more complicated and varied than that, but it is worth considering the additions that some feminists have made to this template. In this reading, it is not only that female and male are biologically opposed, but that their differences contain spiritual and moral elements. Much is made of the ideas of male and female 'energies', of the (unproven) assertion of a male biological drive towards violence, the (equally unproven) assertion of a female biological drive towards compassion, and of the power that lies in the actual or symbolic womb. For all that this comes under a feminist banner, these arguments are strikingly close to Freud's belief that 'biology is destiny', and find their foundations in much of the early white suffrage and temperance movements: the claims that women deserved the vote because they were purer and better than men, that women were not tempted by alcohol because of their innate moral superiority.

The final and, seemingly, most convincing argument is that of socialisation. Trans women, these feminists claim, can never really be women, as the very fact that they needed to transition proves that they were *socialised* as men. At a cursory glance, it makes some sense: who we are is, indeed, predicated to a large degree on what we have been taught to be. Where the anti-trans socialisation argument falls down, though, is in its assumptions about how socialisation works: that it is enacted along some kind of universal binary gendered line, that it is a one-way process, and that it stops after a certain time.

This is to me, as a feminist, abhorrent. It strikes me as wrong not only in its inaccuracy, but in the ways in which it ignores other axes of power and privilege, other ways in which we suffer at each other's hands – the myriad ways in which we benefit from others' suffering, whether we like it or not. I look at my own early years, and see an incredible mix of differing messages, predicated on my family's unique experiences of gender, of nationality, of race and of money and of class, and on my broader cultural positioning within those categories. Many supposed universals of 'female socialisation' were unknown to me, as were those of a supposedly typical male experience. I find commonalities of experience with friends from similar backgrounds, who inhabit similar categories, and I find commonalities with people who, at first glance, would appear to be totally different. There can be – there are – similarities and overlaps of gendered experience, just as there are similarities and overlaps between any cultural groups – but a universal either/or socialisation does not do justice to the multiple nature of inequality and injustice, nor does it help solve these problems. How could I, on the basis of the sex I was assigned at birth, claim to have had the same socialisation as a child born into poverty who has never known what it was like to go to bed well-nourished and safe? The same socialisation as a child denied an education because of warfare, cultural upheaval or a specific localised form of misogyny? To claim that all the privileges of my whiteness matter less than the sex I was assigned at birth, so that my socialisation was that of a child raised with the total violence of embedded racism curtailing their possibilities at every turn? To me, it feels like an insult, an appropriation, to take the experiences of others who have struggled far harder than I ever have had to and say 'this struggle is mine, because of the one way, out of many, we were categorised at birth'.

Neither is socialisation a one-way experience; the human mind is so much more than a blank slate waiting for an outside hand. How someone will hear, interpret and inter-nalise the *multiple* messages they receive, and how they will respond in turn will vary from person to person. To return again to my childhood: a crucial part of my gendered sociali-sation was that I reacted to others' messages as someone who did not feel male or female. Trans people's experiences of how they knew themselves before they had the language to know themselves as trans are hugely diverse, but it would be wrong to assume that we reacted to the gendered mes-sages we received as the sexes we were assigned at birth, or uncomplicatedly so. Trans women who are tarred with the label 'socialised as men' often report childhood experiences of knowing themselves to be girls, of being punished for being feminine, and of being abused for not meeting mascu-line stereotypes. I don't understand how those experiences, both self-reflexive and at the hands of others, constitutes a 'male' socialisation.

Finally we have the idea that it is only socialisation in childhood that matters: that it takes a certain length of time before a person can claim to be a woman or a man, and that if a critical window of opportunity is missed, a person cannot ever 'change gender'. Leaving aside the fact that those putting forth this argument ignore both the existence of young transitioners, and the common occurrence of inner knowledge that predates social transition, this interpretation of how the self is constructed dismisses what we are coming to know of brain plasticity and the evolving field of theory of mind. I know I am not alone in having experienced significant shifts in personality following major life changes in adulthood. My brother's final illness and death altered so much of what I feel to be 'me': my gut reaction to bad news, the length of time it takes me to process difficult emotions, my sleep patterns, the temptation to turn to alcohol in times of pain, the figures that haunt the visions that accompany sleep paralysis, the way that my depressive lows now melt into grieving. My doctor told me that both my immune system and my metabolism were adversely affected by the extreme and ongoing stress. Who I am now is not identical to who I was ten years ago – that's hardly a controversial statement.

Trans-exclusionary radical feminism (as opposed to trans-inclusionary radical feminism) is one strand of feminist practice, but one strand only. Other types of feminism include, but are not limited to: analytic feminism, liberal feminism, postcolonial feminism, black feminism, postmodern feminism, psychoanalytic feminism, anarcho-feminism, Marxist feminism, ecofeminism, intersectional feminism and libertarian feminism. All of these categories contain multiple viewpoints and messages, and many overlap in significant ways. Some are fundamentally opposed to each other, and some share many of the same goals and practices. Feminisms are ever changing, living philosophies and movements.

To be honest, I think the answer to the supposed conflict lies in the broader cultural popularity of infotainment and the twenty-four-hour news cycle. As with any other story, drama and conflict sells.

What are we to do, those of us who want to educate, to learn and to reach out across this divide, but don't want to feed the beast of outrage and ratings and perpetual argument?

I would suggest that we remember that feminisms are more varied, and more valuable, than this one harmful subset. We don't have to play a losing game, or sink to our opponents' levels. Feminism can be for everyone.

American legal scholar and activist Kimberlé Crenshaw put a name to a different way of doing feminism in her writings of the late eighties and early nineties: intersectionality. The first part of the definition given in her 1991 essay, 'Mapping the Margins: Intersectionality, Identity Politics, and Violence Against Women of Color', is one of the most quoted, most easy to understand definitions of this approach available:

> Consider an analogy to traffic in an intersection, coming and going in all four directions. Discrimination, like traffic through an intersection, may flow in one direction, and it may flow in another. If an accident happens in an intersection, it can be caused by cars travelling from any number

of directions and, sometimes, from all of them. Similarly, if a black woman is harmed because she is in the intersection, her injury could result from sex discrimination or race discrimination.

But this definition also comes with a warning, an explanation of what can happen when we deny the ways in which we can be caught at the intersections of our lives:

> ... providing legal relief only when black women show that their claims are based on race or on sex is analogous to calling an ambulance for the victim only after the driver responsible for the injuries is identified. But it is not always easy to reconstruct an accident. Sometimes the skid marks and the injuries simply indicate that they occurred simultaneously, frustrating efforts to determine which driver caused the harm. In these cases the tendency seems to be that no driver is held responsible, no treatment is administered, and the involved parties simply get back in the cars and zoom away.

The objections made to the process of intersectional activism – even to the word itself – run from facile to false. Professional feminist shock jock Julie Burchill likened the word to a bowel complaint, and claimed it was similarly full of shit. A popular media tactic is to claim that intersectionality is a 'made-up' approach, a trend coined by the twitterverse; heavy on pile-ons and the misuse of difficult language, light on actual feminist practice. According to some, the word itself is too long, the idea that some people have more prejudice to contend with than others is too divisive, and the thought of trying to combat multiple, stacking oppressions at the same time is more than our job's worth. In this reading, 'intersectionality' is just a way of trying to make white cis women feel guilty, and naming the whiteness, the cisness of intersectionality's main opponents is identity politics gone mad. 'Intersectional' feminism is what happens on university campuses, where the young and idealistic play oppression Olympics, while the real feminists, the old guard, do the actual work. Supposedly.

I'm not so sure. Not sure how a thirty-year-old word to describe a centuries-old process can be described as new or divisive, certainly – but doubly unsure as to why this kind of feminist process is still being fought over by some when it is an everyday practice for many.

A little while ago I participated in a panel discussion on intersectional feminism in the East End of London. The event had been organised by members of the local council, and both audience and speakers were more varied in their backgrounds, their experiences, than can often be the case at feminist events. For an hour and a half my fellow panel-lists – activists and academics – fielded audience questions, joined in discussion and actively listened to each other. Our differences did not stifle us, but united us in a shared need for learning, communication and support. I learnt a great deal about the ongoing impacts of British colonialism on experiences of gendered oppression and expression. Several older men opened up about what it was like to be forced into a certain type of masculinity; one young woman asked how she could best support trans people while remaining respectful of her Christian background and love of God. It was not hard, or threatening, to learn from one another's experiences:

it was a gift. In considering how we had each benefited from an unfair society, and how we had suffered at its hands, we were not competing to try to find out 'who had it worst' – we were sharing how best to make things fairer for all of us. I don't understand what is controversial, or difficult, about that.

But I do understand what it is to be turned away by the labelling of things when that labelling is unexplained and its processes are unclear. When that label is used to mean a mocking reference to Tumblr teenagers and trigger warnings with everything, with activists who'll delight in tearing down the uninitiated, beginning to understand or practise an intersectional approach might seem intimidating, or pointless.

It is also true that so many guides to intersectional feminism available online point more to the end product than the process. They talk about which words to use, and which points to make, without addressing the fact that words change and goalposts shift. 'Ten ways to make your feminism more intersectional', 'five feminist arguments you didn't realise are cissexist'; quick little lists to read on your phone that can certainly help but rarely delve deeper than 'do this, but not that'. We love to focus on symptoms, but too often leave structures and systems unexamined. Working out how we can do our best by each other is not so simple as just using the most up-to-date terms and, without examining the deepest levels of our thoughts and actions, it can be easy to fall into thinking that intersectionality just means adding a surface layer of 'diversity'. That all you have to do to make your feminism intersectional is to add one photo of a woman in a wheelchair, add one token piece by a trans woman, share an article from a black feminist and call it a day.

I worry about my own tendency towards this. I see the way that others fail me, and know I must, despite my best intentions, be failing others. I need more than just an outcome created by others to be copied: I need an underlying philosophy of my own that can hold me to account, and also inspire me to think more, think harder, and act with greater compassion. I need to think of ways in which, by following this philosophy, I can make it easier for others to develop their own.

I was lucky, then, that the simultaneous publication of two books, and my back-to-back reading of them, helped to clarify these murky and conflicting feelings. The contrast between them, in foundation, in process, in outcome, and my reflection on those contrasts, put into words what it is I want to do with my feminism.

Sheila Jeffreys' *Gender Hurts* and Roxane Gay's *Bad Feminist*: two books from two anglophone feminist writers, each from an influential mainstream publisher, each one from an academic author – Roxane Gay is a Professor of English at Purdue University, while Jeffreys was a Professor of Political Science at the University of Melbourne. Both books told from a queer perspective: Gay is bisexual, Jeffreys a political lesbian. Two different generations, Jeffreys the older and Gay the younger, and two different experiences of racism and racial privilege: Gay is black, Jeffreys is white. Gay's work is a collection of essays, spanning a huge number of topics, while Jeffrey's work is focused on the sole issue of the supposed threat trans people pose to the world in general, and feminism in particular.

Reading *Gender Hurts: A Feminist Analysis of the Politics of Transgenderism* was not a pleasant experience for me – nothing like the evening spent inhaling *Bad Feminist* – but I'm glad that I read both, and in the same day. At each point where Jeffreys' arguments left me feeling excluded, misinterpreted or blamed, Gay's book offered a deeper, more inclusive alternative. The experience left me with four main tenets – ways of questioning my actions and intentions – guides for what my intersectional feminism can be.

Plurality is necessary because there is no neutral

The introduction alone to *Bad Feminist* struck me by its breadth: 'Feminism (n): Plural'. An explicit description of what that means: 'We don't all have to believe in the same feminism. Feminism can be pluralistic so long as we respect the different feminisms we carry along with us, so long as we give enough of a damn to try to minimize the fractures among us.'

Any of us claiming that our feminism is neutral or total is either ignorant or a liar. Even if we do it from the best of intentions – 'this is the *real* feminism, other people claiming to be feminists are cruel and hateful' – it does damage.

So my feminism must remain mine, and I must take responsibility for it, in all the ways in which my insights are valuable and all the ways in which they are limited. In doing so, I can hope to join my voice to others without drowning them out.

Failure is necessary in order to learn

Many of us carry around an image of the 'perfect femi-nist': someone who never makes the 'wrong' choices, always knows what to say, wins every argument, embodies every virtue. Some feminists will take that image so much to heart that they cannot stand to think of the ways in which their real selves fail to measure up.

Gay's solution, in the face of the image of feminist perfection, is to be a 'bad' feminist, because perfection doesn't exist, but trying for something is so much better than nothing. In her essays, she gives herself space to fail and its crucial corollary, space to succeed. The interrogating self is interrogated – both the writer and the reader – but with kindness as well as stringent honesty.

The most important thing I've ever learnt as a musician, both as a student and as a teacher, is that progress is impossible without failure. The trick is to own your mistakes, to own your responsibility for fixing them – and to never stop learning from the example of others.

It might well be the most important part of my feminist learning as well.

We must bring our whole, examined selves to the table

Gay's book certainly has a structural advantage here: personal essays are traditionally more discursive than a quasi-academic text. In combining theory with the little details and human foibles of her daily life, she shows us a realistic version of what it is to be a feminist. Not someone whose every action, every thought, fits a pre-approved template of political righteousness, but a feminist who can tackle the worst problems of our world and still indulge in trashy novels, dubious pop music, drinking too much and worrying about getting it wrong.

There is not one aspect of life where gendered oppression does not reach, and which cannot benefit from feminist inclusion. If we start preemptively cutting out parts of who we are because they're 'not feminist enough', then we've failed before we've begun.

We cannot afford to leave anyone behind

At no point while reading Sheila Jeffreys' work did I have the sensation of being recognised as an equal participant in the feminist movement. Jeffreys talks about the 'politics of transgenderism' rather than trans lives and trans communities. She asserts that people like me are 'created by forces of male power' through 'mutilation' – a reading which is totally at odds with all I know of the trans experience – and seems uninterested in hearing our side of the story. Throughout *Gender Hurts*, I had the sensation of being seen as a problem to be solved, and as a road block in the way of true feminist justice.

I was thankful, then, to come to Gay's words:

Women of color, queer women, and transgender women need to be better included in the feminist project. Women from these groups have been shamefully abandoned by Capital-F Feminism, time and again. This is a hard, painful truth ... For years, I decided feminism was for me as a black woman, as a woman who has been queer identified at varying points in her life, because feminism has, historically, been far more invested in improving the lives of heterosexual white women to the detriment of all others.

And after that reminder, instead of doing down the existence of others in order to prop up her own experiences, Gay writes from the centre out, enriching the understanding of others through the specifics of her own life. Her teaching, her fiction, her experiences of love and hatred, desire, boredom, fear, hope: her narrative is messier and more complicated than Jeffreys', forcing the reader to acknowledge her full humanity – and, from that, the full humanity of others.

Life is seldom perfect, and everyone knows the sometime necessity of a compromise. But if we accept the necessity – the desirability – of offering up the lives of others to improve our own, then we have already lost

My feminism must be intersectional if it is to contain the realities of my trans life, and the lives of all other trans people – trans people whose experiences are often radically different from mine. But it is not only a need for inclusion, and for protection, but a question of feminism's need for all that can be learnt of gender oppression, and of gender itself, in all of its many forms.

Would you like to know the subtle differences between being seen as an effeminate white man and an androgynous white woman? Would you like to know what those differences can do to a person, to their safety, to their comfort, to their ability to move through the world? Ask me – because the world has shown me. Is it only men who enforce gendered norms and enact gendered violence? In my experience it is not, and that experience can be a valuable tool, if we want it to be. If feminism is to help everyone, it has to learn from everyone. The more we learn about the intricacies, overlaps and contrasts of our experiences, the more we can dismantle the totality of gendered oppression.

These extraordinary elements of trans people's collective knowledge – what it is to be the same person perceived in different gendered ways, what it costs to challenge the idea that sex and gender are fixed at birth by outsiders, what it is to exist outside of the gendered system we were taught was universal – how can feminism continue without them? Without the insights of trans women who experience that particular form of oppression, trans misogyny, where they are punished for their womanhood, and punished again for the fact that it is devalued and disbelieved. Without the insights of trans men who, depending on country, race, class, bodies, perceptions, lose and gain any combination of benefits upon transition? Without the accumulated knowledge of those, like me, living outside a gender binary: in the streets, in our homes, in employment, in the social system, in our own minds?

All of this experience, this work, enriches not only our understanding, but gives us all a better skillset with which to fight against the systems that keep us down.

This is the point where, in my experience, some people will say 'Why feminism at all?' 'Doesn't feminism mean female?' 'If you're going to broaden the category, why not call yourself a humanist instead?' For me, that response is yet another of the many reasons why feminism needs trans people. Gendered oppression is so much more than a dualistic fight between women and men, and its cruelties extend beyond one form of discrimination against one group of people. This labelling of the world into things for men, and things for women – good things, bad things – twists what is designated 'womanly', 'feminine', and uses it to punish nearly all of us. Some are hurt far worse than others – but very few make it out unscathed.

We cannot untangle this Gordian knot by pulling on one thread only. We have to stop pretending that, despite acting together, our resources are scarce and our empathy and talents limited. We do not need to pursue only one goal at a time, help only one type of person. The sheer fact of our diversity means we can be diverse in what it is that we need, and what we can do.

Instead of narrowing down our feminist needs and our desires, we could open them up to everyone who has ever had a need to be free of gendered oppression, gender coercion, gendered limitations.

To do this, I need to ask more, expect more, demand more and better. And I need to show myself willing to hear and act on the same demands in turn.

15

Futures

The last hundred years have seen the most extraordinary changes in how society thinks of sex and gender, and trans people have been at the front and centre of these changes. Transition-related medicine has expanded from one sole dedicated gender clinic to a worldwide network of physicians, research facilities and cutting-edge treatments. Trans people in the 1910s were petitioning those in government to plead their cases for them; with the 1999 election of New Zealand MP Georgina Beyer we began to change politics from within. We have gone from being persecuted by the law to, in some places, being protected by it. Trans people have broken ground as scientists, musicians, academics, authors, actors, doctors, parents, charity workers, campaigners – every kind of career and vocation.

And so it's not surprising that *Time* magazine would state that we have come to the 'trans tipping point'. Nor is it surprising that people who aren't trans are eager to talk about how much better things are for people like me – how different, certainly. This sentiment can be presented as something good or something bad, but it is treated as a fact. Sometimes it is in the somewhat hopeful, somewhat fearful predictions of people who care, people whose desire for everything to be equal and sunny makes them determined to see the progress they need to exist. Sometimes it's in the ranting of political pundits, lamenting a world gone mad, a disruption of the natural gendered order. It's the message that much of the mainstream media is invested in recycling, citing its own pronouncements as proof that we exist in a moment of unparalleled trans tolerance and visibility.

The trans people I know are not quite so unified in their opinion. Some, yes, who are happy to broadcast their triumphs, and complain that the real barrier to true trans equality is other trans people, a community tendency to infighting, and a joy in dragging each other down. Others, often older, often reliant on social services, are fearful. They believe that all the tipping point has brought us is the kind of visibility that paints a target on our backs in a time of right-wing backlash and economic instability. Many have marked the difference between the money made by cis writers, producers and editors milking this current trend for trans topics, and the ways in which trans people are pressured by the media into offering up our own lives as 'content' – without recompense. We have never before had so many trans faces in the news. We have never before had such records of overwhelming violence towards trans people.

I try to catch a firm hold of the direction in which we're moving and find myself unable to do so. It depends on the day, on the latest breaking story. Sometimes it comes on a totally personal level: whether a stranger has called me 'they' without needing to be asked or whether I've been catcalled and mocked all the way home. Other times it's in our shifting web of trans communities: a friend beaten up at a bus stop, an acquaintance lost to suicide, a colleague finally being paid and appreciated for their advocacy. I was tearful because of the promise made by First Minister of Scotland Nicola Sturgeon, that her party would pursue legal recognition and protection for people like me. Then tearful again because of yet another description of a trans woman's body beaten and abused beyond recognition, her very existence a threat to be exterminated. Something is happening – something powerful and exhilarating and frequently terrifying – but it is an edge state: I couldn't tell you upon which side we will fall. Trying to balance on that edge is dangerous, exhausting, a constant wash of adrenaline.

The progress, when it comes, is astounding. I see the kind of changes happening now that I imagined, as a teenager, I wouldn't know until the end of my life. Not just in the advances made by trans people, but in the underlying ways in which we consider sex and gender. There is so much to say that, in fact, I am overwhelmed in trying to decide where to start, in what to include and in which order.

Maybe I should begin with the ways in which trans people are finally being recognised in our legitimacies, our talents and our authorities. The University of Victoria has endowed a Chair in Transgender Studies, Dr Aaron Devor, with the aim of linking academic and community-based scholarship, integrating Transgender Studies into a broader curriculum, and maintaining an archive of transgender history. Trans people have long been the subject of academic investigation; increasingly, that scholarship is the product of fellow trans people – a community researching itself – rather than outsiders peering in. The White House has its first trans LGBT Liaison, Raffi Freedman-Gurspan; incredibly, she is the fifth trans appointment of the Obama administration. The total number of trans politicians in the world is on the rise. There are so many I have to pick and choose whose names to report: Emily Brothers in the UK, Geraldine Roman in the Philippines, Tamara Adrián in Venezuela, Kim Coco Iwamoto in Hawaii, Madhu Kinnar in India, Michelle Suárez Bértora in Uruguay, Petra De Sutter in Belgium, Estefania Cortes-Vargas in Canada.

There are an increasing number of trans people playing the media at their own game and winning. Janet Mock's second book is due to arrive in 2017; far from following the 'sell your coming out story and then disappear' media arc all too familiar to trans people, Mock's career as a journalist, presenter and activist grows from strength to strength. Rather than appear as the subject of cis investigation, Mock has established herself as an authoritative investigative voice; her worth lies in what she can do, rather than in how she can be used by others. She is not the only one: the number of trans journalists, trans filmmakers, trans writers and artists of all kinds is growing, and, increasingly, our work is hitting the mainstream. Some are, it's true, pulling the ladder up behind them, but most – whether it's the Wachowski sisters or Laverne Cox – are using their platforms to lift up other trans people and to amplify other voices. Cox knows how to walk a red carpet with the best of them; she also knows how to apply her skills and her fame in the service of justice for other trans women of colour. Musicians like Rae Spoon and Ryan Cassata combine art with advocacy, turning their experiences as trans people into fuel for their music, and reaching out to their own communities to find a fanbase. Instead of having to hide who we are for the slim chance of career advancement, it is increasingly possible, though still difficult, to find success as an openly trans person, and in so doing to chip away at the barriers holding others back.

The younger generation – Generation Z, as they have been dubbed by marketeers and PR firms – frequently demonstrate a trans-positive take on gender, and have the cultural and economic capital to make their elders sit up and take notice. A 2016 study from the USA found that 56 per cent of thirteen- to twenty-year-olds know a person who uses gender-neutral pronouns. Seventy per cent are in favour of gender-neutral bathrooms, and less than half identify as heterosexual. Blurring, disrupting and rejecting traditional gendered models and standards of being and behaviour: far from being the unconsidered trend some older commentators have claimed, at its best this move is part of a broader sense of millennial disenfranchisement with the world we've inherited, and a desire to create something more open and more honest. This championing of gender plurality frequently shows a deep knowledge of how gendered oppression is linked to all other kinds of hatred and bigotry, even as it's expressed through webcomics, emojis and self-referential memes. What is most incredible to me is how unashamed these young people are; I have to admit to moments of envy, thinking how I could never have been so fierce and so unapologetic in my teenaged gender rebellion, no matter how hard I tried. This isn't something confined to subcultures and corners; this showcasing of gender diversity is something taken up by young celebrities, celebrated in selfies and blog posts shared by hundreds of thousands, sometimes millions of people. Seventeen-year-old actor Amandla Stenberg came out as non-binary on her Tumblr page, not as something shocking that needed the intervention of a publicist and a lengthy interview explanation, but as an unabashed part of herself to discuss freely with others like her. The phenomenon that is gender fluid model Ruby Rose has had people of all genders and sexualities questioning what it means to be attracted to androgyny; her popularity has editors reaching for the word 'genderqueer' when they would never have admitted its use before.

It doesn't escape my notice that I'm more likely to find a sensitively written and deeply researched piece on trans lives and trans feminism in *Teen Vogue* or *Seventeen* magazine than I am in the pages of more established and esteemed publications. These two magazines have published pieces on eating disorders in trans teenagers, detailed the prohibitive cost of medical transition, provided guidance on how best to talk to trans friends and have dismantled the myth of the trans bathroom predator. It certainly seems as though the younger generation is leading the way when it comes to compassion and acceptance. Some adult group or service will turn away potential trans members or customers, while the Girl Scouts of the USA refused a $100,000 donation rather than compromise their inclusion of trans scouts. After a Wisconsin school cancelled a reading of young trans activist Jazz Jennings' book, more than 600 people, mostly families with kids, gathered at a local library to show their support for trans children and teenagers. At the LGBTI conferences and meetings I attend, it is more and more common for trans teenagers to be present, usually with their parents and siblings in tow. Like many people, I hang more than a few of my hopes on the open-mindedness of my generation, of the generation that follows.

It would be dangerous, though, to think trans liberation a done deal because of that. In bleaker moments, I have heard fellow activists suggest that the best we can hope for is a future in which the most hateful have died of old age, where this young generation have made good on their promise. In my bleakest moments, I worry that they're right. But that would be a denial not only of the other changes happening around us, but of our responsibility to agitate for those changes, encourage their developments and to guard against pushback. Slower to arrive and far more compromised – but change is coming even in the laws and strictures governing what it is we understand as legal gender categories. The International Olympic Committee has just officially made it easier for trans athletes to compete as their true genders, a move that affects not only the world of sport, but which strikes another blow against the belief that trans people are biological impossibilities, always to be classified as the sex we were assigned at birth. Globally, the recognition that trans people are who we say we are is growing. At the end of 2015 the Vietnamese National Assembly approved a bill to legalise transition-related surgery, and introduce the ability for trans people to be legally recognised. The Swedish government announced that it would be paying compensation to the trans people who underwent enforced sterilisation as a pre-requisite for recognition as their true genders. Canadian Prime Minister Justin Trudeau has promised full equality for trans people, and seems to be working hard to achieve it.

Much of the credit for this increased rate of change must

go to the incredible use of technology by trans activists. Here again I see hope for the future. I cannot imagine a world in which I could have achieved even a quarter of what I've done so far without the use of the internet. Without online information, I wouldn't have learnt about the existence of LGBT school organisations – 'gay-straight alliances' in the terminology of the time – and certainly wouldn't have had the resources with which to found one. Through online forums I found out about other teenagers like me and, together, we founded the first nationwide LGBT group run by and for young people, beginning as an entirely online enterprise. I found friends, support, inspiration, legal advice, a community. Contrary to everything I had seen on television, in the newspapers, I found trans people of every kind struggling, succeeding, thriving. I found my surgeon online; I found a trans artist skilled in body modification. When I could find no 'straight' manager to promote my music, I discovered I already had an online audience who made my career possible. From being alone, we enter into relationships with thousands of other people, sharing the abuses we suffer, but also our victories, working together to make good on both.

The online revolution has allowed trans people to bypass entirely the cis bigots who would deny us a chance at life. As I write this I'm sorting through the most recent fundraising campaigns I've been sent: a campaign to fund a trans modelling agency in Delhi, another to fund a documentary on Slovenian trans culture. The groundbreaking, award-winning film *Tangerine* was filmed on iPhone. Crucially for a community often denied health care and forced into self-medicating, there are online health guides, forums in which to share information: which doctors are the most accepting, how best to get around a broken system, how best to look after a body denied care by the supposed experts. The ability to communicate transparently and in real time is breaking down the ways in which we have been silenced through isolation and through the intimidation of being outnumbered. Every trans conference I have ever been to has been livetweeted for the benefit of those who can't attend in the flesh. Every political action has been reported on from the ground by those involved, broadcasting to a wider network watching at home who stand ready to protest any abuse, and to contact emergency legal aid and support groups.

More than just the change to the practical elements of our shared lives and communities is the change technology has made to the ways in which we interact with each other and see ourselves. The cost – online abuse, doxxing, sustained harassment – is high. But, even with that, the impact is tremendous. I can, if I choose, spend a day speaking with other people, exchanging ideas and sharing the things I love, the things that make me *me*, without ever detailing my gender, the categories into which I am placed. The next day I might choose to tell other people a little about my gendered experiences, but not give them the tools with which to discredit me. Not always, but most of the time, I can find places to be myself and have that self automatically treated as legitimate. That casual allowance of my authenticity is a game changer. Once you get used to it, you never want to go back. I struggled for so long to get the world to accept my correct pronouns: it was only after I had come to expect them, through constant respectful usage online, through trans circles, that I had not just the courage but the expectation to insist on accuracy everywhere. If there is a place where I am treated as truthful, real, desirable even, then I can begin to imagine that that might be true of other places – perhaps of all places. To build a better future we must first be able to imagine it; for many trans people, the internet serves both as our testing ground and as a possibility model of what it would feel like to be so thoroughly accepted as our own selves.

The further we go down the tech rabbit hole, the more we are forced to question our own gendered assumptions – not just trans people, but all of us. Many are accepting the challenge of change, and considering how much further we could go. The improvements to virtual reality technologies are growing exponentially: any appraisal of the current field written here will be out of date the minute I sign off on the text. Still, what we have now leaves me excited, and hopeful. A research project at Universitat Pompeu Fabra in Barcelona has been using the Oculus Rift to allow subjects to 'see' themselves in a differently sexed body. Entitled 'The Machine To Be Another', the project creates a deliberate disjunct between the body known through proprioception and the body seen through the eyes. Subjects have reported feelings of extreme disorientation, a growing awareness of one facet of what trans people experience through dysphoria. I have no doubt that this project will be the first of many and that, no matter how each new technological innovation is presented, there will be those eager to explore each new potential to push open our understanding of empathy, of felt experience, and of what it is to be human. The advent of Artificial Intelligence, too, is no sci-fi scenario; when it comes, will we be prepared to expand what it is that we think we know of humanity, selfhood and the soul?

From the technological to the medical, and the blurring of

these lines; again, the changes multiply at an extraordinary rate. Much of what is reported is exaggerated and distorted through a sensationalistic lens but the innovations in medical technology and research are still staggering. For many trans people, people who experience a burning need to reform their physical bodies, these innovations offer a level of hope impossible to imagine a decade ago. Lili Elbe died in pursuit of a uterine transplant and the possibility of bearing children; 2014 saw the first live birth of a baby born to a mother with a transplanted womb. So far, these transplants have been limited to cis women, but I do not doubt that trials in trans women will follow, though we will have to fight to get there. The news of the growth of rudimentary organs from stem cells was greeted with excitement by many in the trans community; we are a long way from the technologies we would desire, but far closer than we have ever been before. It is not only what these kind of medical treatments could do for trans people and our bodies, but the ways in which these interventions challenge cultural ideas of what is 'natural' and what is helpful. As what was previously seen as impossible and outrageous becomes more normal, it becomes harder to see the changes wrought by transition-related medical care as extreme and unnatural, rather than life-saving and ethical.

It is so easy, from a position of relative safety, to consider these possibilities, to experience these improvements, and in so doing feel that everything is getting better. God knows I feel that pull, particularly when I feel particularly hopeless after one personal struggle or another. Even when we acknowledge the violence, the systemic oppression, experienced by so many, there is the temptation to brush it aside as belonging to the old order of things – an unfortunate relic of another time. When it comes to trans rights, and trans people, I have heard the phrase 'on the wrong side of history' used again and again to describe the people, and the acts, which are rooted in transphobic hatred and fear. They're out of date, out of touch and running out of time.

But that doesn't stop them from hurting us in the here and now. Worse, it allows those who should be helping, who could be doing something, anything, to protect the victims of these violences to turn their backs and say 'it's just not relevant anymore – it'll all be over soon'.

Just as modern and new legislation is designed to protect and recognise trans people, there are still-deadly colonial laws against LGBT people and acts found throughout certain countries, touched by the forces of European imperialism, that prevail. These laws may have been passed in the Victorian era, but are still enforced now, and show every sign of being enforced in the future. The UN notes that private same-sex relationships are criminalised in at least seventy-six countries worldwide. Not all trans people are gay or bisexual, but we are nearly always seen as being queer, and make the most obvious targets for the enforcers of these laws. Elsewhere, new laws are being brought in specifically to target LGBT people, a reflection of broader cultural prejudices and a potent accelerant to existing hatreds; recent anti-LGBT legislative changes in Russia have led to an increase in violence against LGBT people, including a rise in vigilante groups and mob retribution. Sometimes it is the police who target trans people: trans women in Malaysia imprisoned, fined, their heads forcibly shaved for the crime of 'posing as women'. Sometimes it is civilian violence: in January 2016 alone, at least forty-eight Brazilian trans women were murdered. Progress is not inevitable, and any advance can be turned back. An Indonesian Islamic academy for *waria* (loosely analogous to 'trans women'), which had enjoyed great success since opening in 2008, was shut down in 2016 as the result of a sudden and wide-reaching anti-LGBT backlash.

Even in countries where trans people enjoy some protection under law, where we pride ourselves on our 'tolerance', trans people are still suffering. The current rise of austerity politics, political fearmongering and scapegoating have hit trans people hard. The current political chaos, economic downturn and upswing in xenophobic and racist violence in post-Brexit Britain is hitting us even harder. Politicians appealing to the worst and most hateful parts of human nature are lauded as 'hard-hitting', and abusing trans people is an easy way of demonstrating a 'truth-talking', 'un-PC' attitude. Cuts to local services in the UK are putting the most marginalised trans people at risk. In the past year, we have seen the closure of countless community groups that have kept trans people in crisis alive. We have nothing to replace them with. Trans homeless people, trans victims of domestic violence, trans people with mental illnesses, trans children and teenagers: groups like PACE and the Mosaic Youth Centre were the safety net for those who had none. With funding cut and budgets slashed, that safety net is gone, and will not return under this government. The treatment of LGBT asylum seekers should shame us all: desperate people treated like liars, victims of torture told to return to countries where their very existence is a crime. At the time of writing, Theresa May – a politician with an appalling track record on both LGBT rights and the rights of refugees and migrants – is Prime Minister. In times of national upheaval, 'deviants' of all kinds are useful targets for blame. Trans people – particularly trans people of colour, sex workers and disabled trans people – have always made for easy targets.

These are just some of the ways in which trans people are hurting, but these stories do not fit a media narrative of progress, hope and change, and are seldom reported. We are fed the constant message of 'visibility'; that having trans reality TV stars and trans storylines in soap operas is what counts, the word 'gender fluid' used in an ad campaign or a trans model in a special feature in a weekend supplement. It is only in trans activist circles that I have seen this point made: that the trans people most likely to be attacked are already highly visible, and rates of violence against these highly visible people – usually people of colour, usually women, usually sex workers – show no sign of falling. Nearly every gain I could quote for you has its flipside. That backlash is not distributed equally, and those who already suffer the most are inevitably those who are made to suffer more.

When we assume that progress is a done deal, we are turning our backs on those who have experienced no progress at all. When we assume that the arc of history will bend towards justice, we stop working to make it so.

The question I am asked again and again as an activist is: 'What one change would make things better for trans people?' Therein lies the problem. 'Trans' is not a singular quality that can be divorced from the pluralistic lives of the people referred to by that term. Gender diversity, and the need to define one's own gendered place in the world, is a trait found in every human society, every culture, every time and place that I know of. 'Trans' is not a noun but an adjective and a verb, and a shifting, ever-changing one at that. I use the word 'trans' as the broadest and most inclusive term I know of with which to describe the incredible number of ways in which people do gender, and even that is not enough. 'Trans' is a common descriptor worldwide, but there are many specific genders and gendered traditions throughout the world that cannot be parsed by this term, and which lie beyond the scope of this work. And yet these people, too, deserve legal protections, full recognition and freedom from oppression.

I could no more answer the question 'What one thing do trans people need?' than I could 'What one thing do people need?'

Even when I look to myself I know that it will take more than one change to make my life safer and more secure. The current UK Equalities Act makes no provision for people like me. And, yet, that legal protection is nothing without the cultural will to enforce those laws, something any trans woman or trans man could tell me. I wish I had legal documents that accurately recorded who I am, but if that recognition comes at the cost of creating a central registry of trans people then it may well do more harm than good. Better employment laws, better diversity training, a more rigorous desire to promote LGBT equality in education: these are all moves that would have an immediate positive impact on my life. For other trans people, the far more pressing concern is the decriminalisation of sex work: what good is a more inclusive employment law when your work is still liable to result in arrest, police abuse and harassment from social workers? Trans positive health care and trans positive schooling have the potential to help all trans people, but only if they can be freely provided. If I focus my activism upon my own needs I remain ignorant of all the areas in which I am considered 'neutral', which is to say societally favoured.

It is, perhaps, a common tendency to dream of utopias. It's certainly something that drove me into activism and into a desire to write that activism down. When I was much younger I wanted, like many idealists, to create a manifesto: a document both clear and concise, and, of course, universal in its application. With hindsight, it is clear that there can be no such manifesto of trans rights, of trans justice – unless it were to be one without an end, in which anyone could write.

At what point would we be done? When trans people no longer have to undergo sterilisation to be legally recognised? Until medical gatekeeping is replaced with the process of informed consent? Is it enough to insist on the right of gender non-conforming children to be treated with kindness and respect, or do we fight to change the entire process of coercively assigning sex and gendered labels and expectations at birth? Health care, education, the prison system, the justice system, borders and immigration, cultural mores: in every part of society trans people are suffering, and they are suffering in multiple ways. How can we claim to be a community and then insist that it is necessary to leave any one of us behind?

I was talking about this sense of living on the edge, of experiencing backlash, and a colleague stopped me. 'For trans people of colour,' they said, 'it has always been the backlash.' With that, they spun my vision around. Is what we're experiencing now any more or any less vital than the experiences of those at the Compton's Cafeteria riots, or at Stonewall? Is our 'tipping point' greater than all of those tipping points experienced by Magnus Hirschfeld and his trans patients, colleagues and friends? Those may be the public moments of societal debate and obvious change, but what of the millions of personal battles, individual lives poised always between danger and freedom? Each daily struggle to be safe, to be known, to survive, and to ensure safety and survival in the future?

The problem with our trans tipping point is that we think we know which direction it will take us. We assume that our future is already written, and that it must inevitably get better; that the wheels are already in motion, and no longer need fuel to run.

What if, instead, we took responsibility for the danger and the power of these constant edge states? What if we took this moment of public interest and used it to further a future that would benefit us all? If we each took the risk, what could we, collectively, win?

What bears me up, on those days when the backlash and the danger are too much to endure, is the thought of what we might achieve if we can only keep going. I don't believe we can see our final destination from where we are, but our hopes for what it may be are crucial in creating it.

I am working for a future where the fact that some people will make changes to their sexed bodies will be an understandable, and unremarkable, aspect of life, stripped of stigma and shame. Where every child is recognised, valued and loved for their own unique selves. We already have spaces in which we see and respect each other without gendered assumptions and judgements – why shouldn't we expect that everywhere? There is nothing natural or inevitable about the gendered injustices that plague our society – so why should we not imagine a future free of them? One in which our possibilities are limitless and our differences the links in a chain that join us in a common humanity.

If it is truly every movement's goal to make itself obsolete, then I am working for a truly equal future that has no need for the trans movement, having made good on its dreams.

My future might look different from yours – and none of us can predict the exact details of what will come. But I trust that with compassion, empathy, the deep respect for what is unique and special in each of us – the core lesson of trans experience – that it is a future we could all be proud of creating.

We just have to find the courage to try.

Endnotes

1. The Production of Ignorance

1 (and guess who's paying £78k): http://www.express.co.uk/news/uk/220433/Half-man-gets-new-breasts-and-guess-who-s-paying-78k

1 'Monster Chef and the She Male': https://www.buzzfeed.com/lanesainty/the-courier-mails-transphobic-headline-breached-press-counci?utm_term=.qdJj7dvex#.omlvNQPLj

1 'I'm just a bloke, says sex-change soldier': http://www.thetimes.co.uk/tto/news/uk/defence/article4688580.ece

1 'Children as young as FOUR being given transgender lessons': http://www.dailymail.co.uk/news/article-3298715/Children-young-FOUR-given-transgender-lessons-encourage-explore-gender-identities.html

1 'Tran or woman?': https://www.thesun.co.uk/archives/news/393820/tran-or-woman/

1 turned him into a 'monster': http://www.dailymail.co.uk/news/article-2440086/Belgian-transsexual-Nathan-Verhelst-44-elects-die-euthanasia-botched-sex-change-operation.html

2 'The Gender Bender': http://edition.cnn.com/interactive/2014/12/entertainment/cnn10-most-influential/)

2 primary school teacher Lucy Meadows: https://www.theguardian.com/uk/2013/may/28/lucy-meadows-coroner-press-shame

2 before she had transitioned: http://web.archive.org/web/2012 1226073921/http:/www.dailymail.co.uk/debate/article-2251347/Nathan-Uptons-wrong-body-hes-wrong-job.html

3 shame on all of you: https://www.theguardian.com/uk/2013/may/28/lucy-meadows-coroner-press-shame

6   towards genital surgery: http://www.theguardian.com/commentis
    free/2015/oct/14/channel-4-genitalia-surgery-trans-people-girls-to-
    men

7   being denied an answer: http://www.pinknews.co.uk/2014/01/09/
    trans-actress-laverne-cox-a-preoccupation-with-transition-and-
    surgery-objectifies-trans-people/

8   'dicks in chicks clothing': http://www.huffingtonpost.co.uk/planet-
    ivy/julie-burchills-transsexu_b_2478268.html

9   Shakespeare, Austen and Swift: http://www.economist.com/blogs/
    prospero/2014/02/pronouns

10 'Deer spears sex-swap Kate': http://www.pinknews.co.uk/
    2014/05/12/stag-attack-victim-kate-stone-celebrates-removal-of-
    trans-references-from-newspaper-articles

10 'Was Kate gored by stag because she was transgender?: http://
    www.theguardian.com/society/2014/may/11/transgender-kate-stone-
    press-complaints-commission-ruling

14 'Transgender Issues are Driving Me Nuts': http://www.thesunday-
    times.co.uk/sto/comment/columns/jeremyclarkson/article1659305.
    ece

14/15 Y. Gavriel Ansara and Peter Hegarty: http://www.apa.org/monitor/
    2012/09/top-honors.aspx and http://ansaraonline.com/yahoo_site_
    admin/assets/docs/Ansara__Hegarty_2012_Cisgenderism_in_
    Psychology.19690333.pdf

15 'Changing Sex is Not to Be Done Just on a Whim': http://www.
    standard.co.uk/comment/comment/melanie-mcdonagh-changing-
    sex-is-not-to-be-done-just-on-a-whim-a3149031.html

17 'odd', 'gross' and 'freaks': Stephanie Beryl Gazzola and Melanie
    Ann Morrison (2014), 'Cultural and Personally Endorsed
    Stereotypes of Transgender Men and Transgender Women:
    Notable Correspondence or Disjunction?', *International Journal of
    Transgenderism*, 15:2, 76–99, DOI: 10.1080/15532739.2014.937041.

2. 'Call Me Caitlyn'

21 Why didn't Islan Nettles?: http://www.autostraddle.com/what-
    were-going-to-say-about-caitlyn-jenner-292957/

21 'shy, miserable person': https://en.wikipedia.org/wiki/Christine_
    Jorgensen

23 'Did the surgeon's knife make me a woman a woman or a freak':
   Jenni Olson, *The Queer Movie Poster Book*, Chronicle Books, 2004

24 all-out street fight: Susan Stryker, *Transgender History*, Seal Press,
   2008, p. 67.

25 rape, and murder: ibid.

26 stabbing herself to death: http://www.advocate.com/commen-
   tary/2012/12/02/op-ed-how-tv-show-csi-screwing-us-again

26 transgender people, especially women: https://bitchmedia.org/x-
   files-transphobia-transgender-character-weremonster-reboot

28 their body was discovered: http://www.standard.co.uk/news/uk/
   inmates-heard-shouts-of-help-me-before-transexual-prisoner-was-
   found-dead-10053295.html

28 National Offender Management Service Deaths in Custody
   Database: https://www.gov.uk/government/uploads/system/uploads/
   attachment_data/file/493975/deaths-in-custody-table.pdf

3. Finding My Voice

38 in the front as feminine: Sonja K. Foss, Mary E. Domenico and
   Karen A. Foss, *Gender Stories: Negotiating Identity in a Binary World*,
   Waveland Press, 2013 p. 135.

4. Couldn't You Just ... Not Be?

48 and other service providers: Jaime M. Grant, Lisa A. Mottet, Justin
   Tanis, Jack Harrison, Jody L. Herman and Mara Keisling, Injustice
   at Every Turn: A Report of the National Transgender Discrimination
   Survey. Washington: National Center for Transgender Equality and
   National Gay and Lesbian Task Force, 2011.

48 a terrifying combination: ibid.

49 a hard-to-reach goal: 'Being Trans in the European Union:
   Comparative analysis of EU LGBT survey data', produced by the
   European Union Agency for Fundamental Rights, 2014.

52 the mercy of individual doctors: http://www.theguardian.com/
   society/2015/may/20/nhs-treats-transgender-people-as-second-
   class-citizens-says-watchdog

52 in India: Yadavendra Singh, Abhina Aher, Simran Shaikh, Sonal
   Mehta, James Robertson and Venkatesan Chakrapani (2014),

'Gender Transition Services for Hijras and Other Male-to-Female Transgender People in India: Availability and Barriers to Access and Use', *International Journal of Transgenderism*, 15: 1, 1–15, DOI: 10.1080/15532739.2014.890559.

52   Colombia: Rodrigo A. Aguayo-Romero, Carol A. Reisen, Maria Cecilia Zea, Fernanda T. Bianchi and Paul J. Poppen (2015), 'Gender Affirmation and Body Modification Among Transgender Persons in Bogotá, Colombia', *International Journal of Transgenderism*, 16:2, 103–115, DOI: 10.1080/15532739.2015.1075930.

52   the Philippines: Sam Winter PhD , Sass Rogando-Sasot and Mark King PhD (2007), 'Transgendered Women of the Philippines', *International Journal of Transgenderism*, 10:2, 79–90, DOI: 10.1080/15532730802182185.

53   to make them larger: Katie Sutton, '"We Too Deserve a Place in the Sun": The Politics of Transvestite Identity in Weimar Germany', *German Studies Review* 35, no. 2 (May 2012): 335–54.

53   all of these methods: https://gidreform.wordpress.com/2008/11/26/the-gender-gulag-voices-of-the-asylum/

55   the study was based: Vern L. Bullough PhD and DSci abd RN (2007), 'Legitimatizing Transsexualism', *International Journal of Transgenderism*, 10:1, 3–13, DOI: 10.1300/ J485v10n01_02.

5. What About Sex?

61   of even five categories: http://capone.mtsu.edu/phollowa/5sexes.html

63   of having green eyes: http://intersexroadshow.blogspot.co.uk/2012/03/how-common-is-intersex-status.html

66   nor is X that of femininity: http://www.newstatesman.com/future-proof/2015/02/sex-isn-t-chromosomes-story-century-misconceptions-about-x-y

67   So why focus on difference?: Cordelia Fine, *Delusions of Gender: the real science behind sex differences*, Icon Books, 2007, p. 165.

69   XY chromosomes: http://www.nature.com/news/sex-redefined-1.16943

72   was wholly jarring …: Julia Serano, *Whipping Girl: A Transsexual Woman on Sexism and the Scapegoating of Femininity*, Seal Press, 2007, pp. 80–87.

75 falling in the middle: Laura Gowing, 'Lesbians and Their Like in Early Modern Europe, 1500–1800', in ed. Robert Aldrich, *Gay Life & Culture: a world history*, Thames & Hudson, 2006.

75 gendered behaviour must be policed: Kathryn M. Ringrose, 'Living in the Shadows: Eunuchs and Gender in Byzantium', in ed. Gilbert Herdt, *Third Sex, Third Gender: Beyond Sexual Dimorphism in Culture and History*, Zone Books, 1994.

74 Laura Gowing, p. 129.

76 in a straight line: Graham Robb, *Strangers: Homosexual Love in the Nineteenth Century*, Picador, 2004, p. 46.

78 as recently as 1979: https://news.google.com/newspapers?id=HUw NAAAAIBAJ&sjid=OG0DAAAAIBAJ&pg=3534,407368&dq=ban gladesh&hl=en

78 'this preference has an evolutionary advantage behind it': http:// content.time.com/time/health/article/0,8599,1654371,00.html

79 (daintier and more delicate): https://www.theguardian.com/science/ 2007/aug/25/genderissues

6. Think of the Children

83 transgender children: http://www.slate.com/blogs/outward/2016/01/14/ what_alarmist_articles_about_transgender_children_get_wrong.html

84 to feel as they did: Natacha Kennedy http://www.academia. edu/2760086/Transgender_Children_More_than_a_Theoretical_ Challenge_2012_updated_version_

89 the general population: http://www.huffingtonpost.com/brynn- tannehill/the-end-of-the-desistance_b_8903690.html

90 without fear of rejection: http://www.huffingtonpost.com/brynn- tannehill/the-end-of-the-desistance_b_8903690.html

92 about delaying puberty or transitioning: Zack Ford, 'This is What Happens to Transgender Kids Who Delay Puberty', Think Progress, LGBT, 16 September, 2014 8:55 AM.

92 across the board: http://www.eurekalert.org/pub_releases/2015-03/ tes-sdc030615.php

92 another six years to complete: http://www.nature.com/news/ largest-ever-study-of-transgender-teenagers-set-to-kick-off- 1.19637

7. Delusional and Disturbed

99 dress and act like women: Graham Robb, *Strangers: Homosexual Love in the Nineteenth Century*, p. 43.

99 sodium pentothal and testosterone: http://www.liverpoolmuseums. org.uk/mol/exhibitions/april-ashley/early-life.aspx

8. A Different Approach

103 trans children without that support: Impacts of Strong Parental Support for Trans Youth. A report prepared for Children's Aid Society of Toronto and Delisle Youth Service Trans Pulse Building our communities through research, 2012.

103 group of young people: http://www.seattletimes.com/seattle-news/ health/family-support-boosts-transgender-kids-mental-health-uw-study-finds/

10. Are Trans People Real?

118 'the "trans" pantomime': http://www.gaystarnews.com/article/ richard-littlejohn-transphobic-rant/#gs.AzMF7LU

119 anti-trans bathroom bill in 2016: http://www.theatlantic.com/poli-tics/archive/2016/05/hb2-is-a-constitutional-monstrosity/482106/

119 bills soon after: http://www.advocate.com/transgender/2016/2/25/ republican-national-committee-endorses-anti-trans-bathroom-bills

119 capitulating to popular anti-trans sentiment: http://www.nytimes. com/2017/06/12/magazine/the-long-lonely-road-of-chelsea-manning.html

119 in their own homes: http://thinkprogress.org/lgbt/2016/04/26/ 3772708/ted-cruz-transgender-bathrooms-at-home/

119 by trans bathroom predators: http://www.slate.com/blogs/ outward/2016/05/11/north_carolina_school_board_allows_pepper_ spray_against_trans_students.html

119 after widespread condemnation: http://www.independenttribune. com/news/rowan-salisbury-school-board-decides-not-to-allow-pepper-spray/article_4af1e660-21af-11e6-aa7c-5318d9219a48.html

119 fend off trans people: http://www.advocate.com/transgender/ 2016/4/25/right-wingers-pledge-carry-guns-bathroom-fend-trans-folks

119 that best match our genders: http://www.usatoday.com/story/money/

2016/04/25/conservative-christian-group-boycotting-target-transgender-bathroom-policy/83491396/

121   after gym class: http://time.com/3905462/mike-huckabee-transgender-joke/

123   with a razor: http://www.advocate.com/politics/transgender/2015/03/31/incarcerated-texas-trans-woman-finally-wins-safer-housing-after-repe

123   for over a decade: https://news.vice.com/article/transgender-offenders-are-being-victimized-in-jails-across-the-world-and-justice-systems-cant-cope

123   Vicky Thompson in 2015: http://www.independent.co.uk/news/uk/crime/death-of-transgender-woman-vicky-thompson-in-male-prison-prompts-calls-for-law-change-a6742676.html

123   denied her medication: http://www.independent.co.uk/news/world/americas/black-transgender-woman-breaks-down-in-interview-over-her-abuse-in-prison-a6870566.html

124   recently attempted suicide: http://www.aljazeera.com/news/2016/07/lawyers-confirm-chelsea-manning-attempted-suicide-160712055644219.html

124   their lived gender: http://www.bbc.co.uk/news/uk-34984249

126   'Oh, my God, that's disgusting': https://en.wikipedia.org/wiki/Quagmire%27s_Dad

127   an undisclosed sum: https://en.wikipedia.org/wiki/There%27s_Something_About_Miriam

128   Gwen's trans status: http://www.sfgate.com/bayarea/article/hayward-defense-calls-transgender-victim-guilty-2792421.php

128   their appalling brutality: https://www.hrw.org/report/2014/10/21/not-safe-home/violence-and-discrimination-against-lgbt-people-jamaica

128   They get aggressive and kill the sex worker: http://www.vice.com/en_uk/read/most-dangerous-place-transgender-europe-turkey-didem-tali

128   against trans people: http://www.vox.com/2015/10/20/9574239/transgender-murders-epidemic

129   And they will be missed: http://www.advocate.com/transgender/2015/08/25/watch-janets-mocks-powerful-response-murders-trans-women

129   *a woman avoids jail*: https://www.theguardian.com/uk-news/2015/dec/15/woman-who-used-fake-penis-to-have-sex-with-a-woman-avoids-jail

129   *reveals her horror*: http://www.thesun.co.uk/sol/homepage/news/6806667/Mum-duped-into-sex-by-lesbian-posing-as-a-man-blasts-judge-for-jail-let-off.html

129   *she met on Facebook*: http://www.lincolnshireecho.co.uk/Lincolnshire-woman-posed-man-sexually-assaulted/story-28069633-detail/story.html

130   'selfish ... dreadful and deceitful': http://www.theguardian.com/uk-news/2015/dec/15/woman-who-used-fake-penis-to-have-sex-with-a-woman-avoids-jail

133   Norway and Ireland: http://www.theguardian.com/world/2015/jul/16/ireland-transgender-law-gender-recognition-bill-passed

11. The Denial of History

139   found throughout the text: Nerissa Gailey and AD Brown, 'Beyond Either/or: Reading Trans* Lesbian Identities', *Journal of Lesbian Studies* 20, no. 1 (2015): 65–86.

142   I have ever seen: Helen Russell, 'Gerda Wegener: "The Lady Gaga of the 1920s"', *Guardian* (London), 28 September 2015.

143   with police permission: Graham Robb, *Strangers: Homosexual Love in the Nineteenth Century*, p. 166.

143   the Prussian state?: Vern L. Bullough PhD and DSci abd RN (2007), 'Legitimatizing Transsexualism', *International Journal of Transgenderism*, 10:1, 3–13, DOI: 10.1300/ J485v10n01_02 (p. 5).

144   and 'homosexual': Susan Stryker, *Transgender History*, p. 38.

144   'the most dangerous Jew in Germany': Florence Tamagne, 'The Homosexual Age, 1870–1940', in *Gay Life & Culture*.

144   World League for Sexual Reform: Susan Stryker, *Transgender History*.

145   pushing a kink too far: Brett Genny Beemyn, 'A Presence in the Past: A Transgender Historiography', *Journal of Women's History*, 2013.

145   silent movie adaptation: https://en.wikipedia.org/wiki/Karl_M._Baer

145   surgical transition in 1917: https://en.wikipedia.org/wiki/Alan_L._Hart

145   this nature were performed: We too deserve a place in the sun.

146   a complete woman: We too deserve a place in the sun.

149   numbers were considerable: Florence Tamagne, 'The Homosexual Age, 1870–1940', in *Gay Life & Culture*.

149   further punishment for their 'crimes': https://en.wikipedia.org/wiki/Paragraph_175#The_Nazi_era

12. Beyond Binaries

152   the category contained multitudes: Kathryn M. Ringrose, 'Living in the Shadows: Eunuchs and Gender in Byzantium', in *Third Sex, Third Gender*.

154   to become a pederast: Casanova, quoted by Vern L. and Bonnie Bullough, *Cross Dressing, Sex, and Gender*, University of Pennsylvania Press, 1993, pp. 84–5.

155/156 and femininity of movement: Theo van de Meer, 'Sodomy and the Pursuit of a Third Sex in Early Modern Europe', in *Third Sex, Third Gender*.

156   the object of everybody: Michael Sibalis, 'Male Homosexuality in the Age of Enlightenment and Revolution, 1680–1850', in *Gay Life & Culture*.

157   as women gave them: Bernd-Ulrich Hergemöller, 'The Middle Ages', in *Gay Life & Culture*.

158   executed by beheading: Laura Gowing, 'Lesbians and Their Like in Early Modern Europe, 1500-1800', in *Gay Life & Culture*.

160   any specific detriment: https://petition.parliament.uk/petitions/104639

160   to the Ministry of Justice: https://drive.google.com/file/d/0B6uo3Mt-MvPfa1R6X05zckVlX2VUMyliMFZCWUhMWEdoUk1Z/view

160   at the beginning of 2016: https://www.parliament.uk/business/committees/committees-a-z/commons-select/women-and-equalities-committee/inquiries/parliament-2015/transgender-equality/

160   dismissed it: https://www.gov.uk/government/uploads/system/uploads/attachment_data/file/535764/Government_Response_to_the_Women_and_Equalities_Committee_Report_on_Transgender_Equality.pdf

160   or government official: http://fusion.net/story/294831/maria-munir-non-binary-gender-comes-out-president-obama/

161   gendered categories: http://www.pinknews.co.uk/2016/02/10/will-smith-is-proud-that-fearless-jaden-wears-womens-clothes/

161   reported such feelings: http://people.socsci.tau.ac.il/mu/daphna-joel/files/2014/11/Joel_gender_identity_2013.pdf

161   between male and female: Non-binary gender factsheet, M-J Barker, CN Lester (2015): http://rewriting-the-rules.com/non-binary-gender-factsheet-

13. The T from the LGB

166 broader term 'queer': Greta R. Bauer, Nik Redman, Kaitlin Bradley and Ayden I. Scheim. 'Sexual Health of Trans Men Who Are Gay, Bisexual, or Who Have Sex with Men: Results from Ontario, Canada.' *International Journal of Transgenderism* 14, no. 2 (2013): 66–74.

166 their sexual orientation: Scottish Trans Alliance 2012 trans mental health.

168 these modern ideas grew: Brett Genny Beemyn, 'The Americas: From Colonial Times to the 20th Century', in *Gay Life & Culture*.

168 'a woman's soul trapped in the wrong body': Florence Tamagne, 'The Homosexual Age, 1870–1940', in *Gay Life & Culture*.

170 same-sex-oriented man: Gert Hekma, '"A Female Soul in a Male Body": Sexual Inversion as Gender Inversion in Nineteenth-Century Sexology', *Third Sex, Third Gender: Beyond Sexual Dimorphism in Culture and History*, edited by Gilbert H. Herdt, Zone Books, 1996.

171 despite his birth: Louis Sullivan, *From Female to Male: the life of Jack Bee Garland*, Alyson Publications, 1990.

172 and sacrificial victims: Susan Stryker, *Transgender History*.

174 For me, pronouns: https://en.wikipedia.org/wiki/Leslie_Feinberg and https://www.nytimes.com/2014/11/25/nyregion/leslie-feinberg-writer-and-transgender-activist-dies-at-65.html?_r=0

174 She died in 2014: http://www.advocate.com/arts-entertainment/books/2014/11/17/transgender-pioneer-leslie-feinberg-stone-butch-blues-has-died

175 what is woman?: p. 117/118, *S/He*, Minnie Bruce Pratt, Alyson Publications, 2005.

14. Trans Feminisms

179 our feminisms are stuck: Gabrielle Le Roux, 'Proudly African and Transgender', *Women: A Cultural Review*, 2012.

179 *in bitter debate*': http://www.smh.com.au/national/what-makes-a-woman-feminists-take-on-transgender-community-in-bitter-debate-20151113-gkyk6u.html

180 *radical feminism and transgenderism*: http://www.newyorker.com/magazine/2014/08/04/woman-2

180 *Feminism and the Transgender Movement*: http://www.morning

staronline.co.uk/a-cb92-The-conflict-between-feminism-and-the-transgender-movement

180 *What makes a woman?:* http://www.ibtimes.co.uk/transgender-rights-versus-feminism-what-makes-woman-1501487

187 or race discrimination: Collected in Helma Lutz, Maria Teresa, Herrera Vivar and Linda Supik (eds.), *Framing Intersectionality: Debates on a Multi-Faceted Concept in Gender Studies*, Ashgate, Taylor and Francis, 2011; "Demarginalising the Intersection of Race and Sex: A Black Feminist Critique of Anti-discrimination Doctrine, Feminist Theory, and Anti-racist Politics" by Kimberlé W. Crenshaw

187 and zoom away: ibid

187 was similarly full of shit: http://www.spectator.co.uk/2014/02/dont-you-dare-tell-me-to-check-my-privilege/

191 'Feminism (n): Plural': Roxane Gay, *Bad Feminist*, Corsair, 2014, p. iv.

191 he fractures among us: ibid., p. xiii.

193 'created by forces of male power': Sheila Jeffreys, *Gender Hurts*, Routledge, 2014, p. 20.

193 to the detriment of all others: Roxane Gay, *Bad Feminist* (introduction), p. xiii.

15. Futures

199 a Chair in Transgender Studies: http://www.uvic.ca/research/transchair/

200 the Obama administration: http://www.advocate.com/transgender/2016/3/14/latina-just-became-first-transgender-white-house-lgbt-liaison

200 to arrive in 2017: http://www.publishersweekly.com/pw/by-topic/industry-news/book-deals/article/69778-book-deals-week-of-march-28-2016.html

201 identify as heterosexual: https://broadly.vice.com/en_us/article/teens-these-days-are-queer-af-new-study-says

202 trans teenagers: http://www.teenvogue.com/story/transgender-youth-eating-disorders

202 of medical transition: http://www.teenvogue.com/story/transgender-operations-hormone-therapy-costs

202 to trans friends: http://www.teenvogue.com/story/things-to-never-ask-transgender-people-hari-nef

202 bathroom predator: http://www.seventeen.com/life/school/news/

a31352/in-unsurprising-news-trans-students-have-caused-zero-incidents-in-public-bathrooms/

202   inclusion of trans scouts: http://www.huffingtonpost.com/entry/girl-scouts-transgender-donation_us_5592d41fe4b000c99eelcc65

202   children and teenagers: http://www.hrc.org/blog/heartwarming-story-of-the-day-outpouring-of-support-for-transgender-youth-i

203   assigned at birth: http://www.telegraph.co.uk/sport/olympics/12120061/Transgender-athletes-allowed-to-compete-at-Rio-Olympics-without-sex-reassignment-surgery.html

203   legally recognised: https://www.hrw.org/news/2015/11/30/vietnam-positive-step-transgender-rights

203   their true genders: http://tgeu.org/trans-people-to-receive-compensation-for-forced-sterilisation-in-sweden/

203   working hard to achieve it: http://www.washingtontimes.com/news/2016/may/23/justin-trudeau-canadian-prime-minister-seeks-feder/

206   a differently sexed body: http://www.wired.com/2014/02/crazy-oculus-rift-experiment-lets-men-women-swap-bodies/

207   transplanted womb: http://www.abc.net.au/news/2014-10-04/woman-has-baby-after-womb-transplant-in-sweden/5790726

207   from stem cells: http://www.nbcnews.com/health/health-news/researchers-grow-kidney-intestine-stem-cells-n441066

208   and mob retribution: https://www.hrw.org/report/2014/12/15/license-harm/violence-and-harassment-against-lgbt-people-and-activists-russia

208   'posing as women': https://www.hrw.org/report/2014/09/24/im-scared-be-woman/human-rights-abuses-against-transgender-people-malaysia

208/209 trans women were murdered: http://feministing.com/2016/02/03/at-least-48-transgender-women-killed-in-brazil-in-january/

209   anti-LGBT backlash: http://www.buzzfeed.com/lesterfeder/muslim-school-for-trans-women-shut-down-in-indonesia#.wo0vb5qaZ

209   those who had none: http://www.theguardian.com/society/2016/feb/02/services-for-lgbt-young-people-will-just-disappear

209   very existence is a crime: https://www.freemovement.org.uk/lgbt-asylum-seekers-a-toxic-mix-of-homophobia-misogyny-and-ignorance-corrupts-the-asylum-system/

Further Resources

Organisations and Campaigns

International
ILGA – International Lesbian, Gay, bisexual, trans and intersex Association
http://ilga.org/
Global umbrella organisation for 1,200 national and international organisations working for LGBTI rights. Research, resources, conferences and
campaigning.
TGEU – Transgender Europe
http://tgeu.org/
Pan-European campaigning and research organisation. Extensive
resources for trans people living throughout Europe, and links with
international groups and campaigns.
United Nations Free & Equal Campaign
https://www.unfe.org/
Public education campaign to promote global LGBT equality. Fact sheets,
films and outreach.

UK
Scottish Transgender Alliance
http://www.scottishtrans.org/
Scottish-based organisation campaigning for equality for all gender diverse
people. Research, resources, outreach and support.
Gendered Intelligence
http://genderedintelligence.co.uk/
Supporting trans youth, and their families, friends and teachers. Resources,
research, youth groups, educational outreach and arts projects.

Books

Redefining Realness
Janet Mock
(New York: Atria Books, 2014)
Bestselling memoir from leading US trans activist and journalist

Gender Outlaws: The Next Generation
Kate Bornstein and S. Bear Bergman
(Berkeley, California: Seal Press, 2010)
Essays, comics, conversation and commentary from the new trans generation

Stone Butch Blues
Leslie Feinberg
www.lesliefeinberg.net (New edition available for free)
Classic novel about growing up different in a binary gendered world

One in Every Crowd
Ivan Coyote
(Vancouver, BC: Arsenal Pulp Press, 2012)
Anthology of stories for young LGBT people

Trans Bodies, Trans Selves
Edited by Laura Erickson-Schroth
(Oxford; New York: Oxford University Press, USA, 2014)
A life guide for trans people: health, relationships, family, employment,
    and more

Film and TV

Her Story
http://www.herstoryshow.com/
Emmy-nominated web series follow the lives of two trans women, their
    colleagues, lovers, and friends

My Genderation
http://www.mygenderation.com/
Short films showcasing trans life in the UK

Paris is Burning
Acclaimed documentary chronicling the ball culture of New York's black
    and Latinx trans and queer communities

Acknowledgements

My deepest thanks, first and foremost, to every trans person who has helped me through the years and ways leading towards the writing of this book. Thank you for the validation, the laughter, the sense of hope and belonging – and thank you also for the challenges, discussions, and the constant push to do better by each other. They are invaluable gifts.

My thanks and gratitude to the team at Virago, particularly Lennie Goodings and Ailah Ahmed, for believing in this work and this author, and for all of their advice, guidance and support. It means a great deal.

To my agent Laura Macdougall, deepest thanks – for your vision, your clarity, and the incredible support. Thank you also to the whole of Tibor Jones, and to Kaite Welsh, who started the ball rolling.

I am grateful to Ruth and Ben, not only for their feedback on the manuscript, but also for their inspirational work in academia and activism. Any mistakes are, of course, my own.

To the friends and family who provided sounding boards, feedback, and much-needed moral support: there would be no book without you. Thank you so very much.

And, finally, especial thanks to my partner Sam, for everything.

And to Jonathan – always.

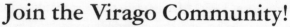 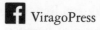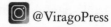
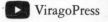